The Political Culture of Nordic Self-Understanding

T0314846

'Power investigation', or the practice of power to legitimize itself through commissioned programmes of scientific enquiry, is a hallmark of Nordic democracy. Five power investigations have been conducted in the Nordic countries since 1972. The close connection to state power has not dissuaded prominent scholars from participating in them, nor have their findings evoked strong criticism. Combining politically guided perspectives with collaborative research, power investigations represent public events that typify the ostensibly open political culture of the Nordic countries, rather than simply existing as texts or as a politico-scientific genre. Although such investigations have been thought of as critical studies of power, the authors in this book show that their findings have varied greatly and that they have served as tools for wielding power. Whatever shortcomings they uncover, the utility of these investigations in suggesting transparency and self-reflection enhances the legitimacy of Scandinavian government. The investigations are persuasive exercises through which the commissioning authorities and those scholars hired to carry them out engage in a mutually beneficial exchange. Underlying this strategy is the perception, deeply embedded in Nordic political culture, that politics is a progressive, rational endeavour, and that identification with the state is an honourable role for academics.

This book was originally published as a special issue of the *Journal of Contemporary European Studies*.

Ainur Elmgren is a Post-doctoral Researcher in Political Science and History at the Network for European Studies, University of Helsinki, Finland.

Norbert Götz is Professor of History at the Institute of Contemporary History, Södertörn University, Sweden.

The Political Culture of Nordic Self-Understanding

Power investigation

Edited by
Ainur Elmgren and Norbert Götz

Routledge
Taylor & Francis Group

LONDON AND NEW YORK

First published 2016
by Routledge
2 Park Square, Milton Park, Abingdon, Oxon, OX14 4RN, UK

and by Routledge
711 Third Avenue, New York, NY 10017, USA

First issued in paperback 2017

Routledge is an imprint of the Taylor & Francis Group, an informa business

British Library Cataloguing in Publication Data
A catalogue record for this book is available from the British Library

ISBN 13: 978-1-138-09923-4 (pbk)
ISBN 13: 978-1-138-93919-6 (hbk)

Typeset in Times New Roman
by RefineCatch Limited, Bungay, Suffolk

Publisher's Note
The publisher accepts responsibility for any inconsistencies that may have arisen during the conversion of this book from journal articles to book chapters, namely the possible inclusion of journal terminology.

Disclaimer
Every effort has been made to contact copyright holders for their permission to reprint material in this book. The publishers would be grateful to hear from any copyright holder who is not here acknowledged and will undertake to rectify any errors or omissions in future editions of this book.

Contents

Citation Information   vii

Notes on Contributors   ix

1. 'Power Investigation: The Political Culture of Nordic Self-Understanding':
   Introduction   1
   Ainur Elmgren & Norbert Götz

2. Introspective Performance: The Scandinavian Power Investigation as a
   Politico-Cultural Practice   4
   Norbert Götz

3. From the Swedish Model to the Open Society: The Swedish Power
   Investigation and the Power to Investigate Power, 1985–1990   20
   Carl Marklund

4. Three Nordic Power Investigations on the Repercussions of the European
   Union on Sovereignty and Democracy   35
   Ann-Cathrine Jungar

5. 'Power Investigation' Neglected: The Case of the Finnish Newspaper
   Helsingin Sanomat   45
   Lotta Lounasmeri

6. Power and Society in Finland: Change and Continuity   60
   Ainur Elmgren

7. Justice and EU Foreign Policy   76
   Alex Prichard

8. Informal Governance and the Eurozone Crisis   93
   Alexandra Hennessy

Index   111

Citation Information

The chapters in this book were originally published in the *Journal of Contemporary European Studies*, volume 21, issue 3 (September 2013). When citing this material, please use the original page numbering for each article, as follows:

Chapter 1
'Power Investigation: The Political Culture of Nordic Self-Understanding':
Introduction
Ainur Elmgren & Norbert Götz
Journal of Contemporary European Studies, volume 21, issue 3 (September 2013)
pp. 338–340

Chapter 2
Introspective Performance: The Scandinavian Power Investigation as a Politico-
Cultural Practice
Norbert Götz
Journal of Contemporary European Studies, volume 21, issue 3 (September 2013)
pp. 341–356

Chapter 3
From the Swedish Model to the Open Society: The Swedish Power Investigation and
the Power to Investigate Power, 1985–1990
Carl Marklund
Journal of Contemporary European Studies, volume 21, issue 3 (September 2013)
pp. 357–371

Chapter 4
Three Nordic Power Investigations on the Repercussions of the European Union on
Sovereignty and Democracy
Ann-Cathrine Jungar
Journal of Contemporary European Studies, volume 21, issue 3 (September 2013)
pp. 372–381

Chapter 5

'Power Investigation' Neglected: The Case of the Finnish Newspaper Helsingin Sanomat
Lotta Lounasmeri
Journal of Contemporary European Studies, volume 21, issue 3 (September 2013)
pp. 382–396

Chapter 6

Power and Society in Finland: Change and Continuity
Ainur Elmgren
Journal of Contemporary European Studies, volume 21, issue 3 (September 2013)
pp. 397–412

Chapter 7

Justice and EU Foreign Policy
Alex Prichard
Journal of Contemporary European Studies, volume 21, issue 3 (September 2013)
pp. 413–429

Chapter 8

Informal Governance and the Eurozone Crisis
Alexandra Hennessy
Journal of Contemporary European Studies, volume 21, issue 3 (September 2013)
pp. 430–447

For any permission-related enquiries please visit:
http://www.tandfonline.com/page/help/permissions

Notes on Contributors

Ainur Elmgren is a Post-doctoral Researcher in Political Science and History at the Network for European Studies, University of Helsinki, Finland.

Norbert Götz is Professor of History at the Institute of Contemporary History, Södertörn University, Sweden.

Alexandra Hennessy is Assistant Professor in the Department of Political Science and Public Affairs at Seton Hall University, New Jersey, USA.

Ann-Cathrine Jungar is Associate Professor of Political Science at Södertörn University, Sweden.

Lotta Lounasmeri is a Post-doctoral Fellow in Media and Communication Studies at the University of Helsinki, Finland.

Carl Marklund is a Post-doctoral Researcher at the Centre for Baltic and East European Studies at Södertörn University, Sweden.

Alex Prichard is Lecturer in the Department of Politics, University of Exeter, UK.

INTRODUCTION

'Power Investigation: The Political Culture of Nordic Self-Understanding': Introduction

AINUR ELMGREN[a] & NORBERT GÖTZ[b]

[a]*Network for European Studies, University of Helsinki, Finland,* [b]*Centre for Nordic Studies, University of Helsinki, Finland*

'Power investigation', or the need for power to renew and legitimize itself through public self-reflection and self-criticism, has a long history in northern Europe. The tradition has been traced, especially by Norwegian commentators to the *Heimskringla*, an Icelandic collection of sagas on Norse kings written in the thirteenth century. A modern tradition of investigating power and its effects on society has emerged in the twentieth century, with the first power investigation in the present sense initiated by the Norwegian government in 1972. It in turn inspired similar endeavours in the other Scandinavian countries in the decades that followed. The most recent power investigation was concluded in Finland in 2010.

All Nordic power investigations have been motivated as responses to perceived changes in society, politics, and the economy. The investigations of the 1970s and 1980s were triggered by increasing criticism directed towards the welfare state and the desire of the Social Democratic parties of Norway and Sweden to come to terms with the decline of their political hegemony. Fears of bureaucratic stagnation were tempered by attempts to integrate the concepts of liberty and openness into the discourse of the welfare state. In the 1990s and 2000s, conservative and liberal parties continued along this path, where Europeanization and internationalization of policy-making were conceived as mounting challenges to be addressed by power investigations.

Five power investigations have been conducted in the Nordic countries since 1972, and they constitute a unique body of scholarly work. The close connection of these investigations to state power has not dissuaded prominent scholars from participating in them, nor have their findings evoked strong criticism. Combining politically guided perspectives with collaborative research, power investigations represent public events that typify the ostensibly open political culture of the Nordic countries, rather than simply existing as texts or a genre. Although such investigations have been thought of as critical studies of power, the articles in this special issue suggest that they are also tools for wielding power. Whatever shortcomings they may uncover in their respective countries, the utility of these investigations in suggesting transparency and self-reflection enhances the legitimacy of Scandinavian government. The investigations are persuasive exercises through which the commissioning authorities and those scholars hired to carry them out engage in a mutually beneficial exchange. Underlying this strategy is the perception, deeply embedded in Nordic political culture, that politics is a progressive, rational endeavour, and that identification with the state is an honourable role for scholars.

VALTA,[1] a multidisciplinary research programme on power conducted in Finland, is the latest of such investigations, but it is distinctive from the others in crucial ways. The VALTA programme, which has recently undergone its final evaluation, offers a particular occasion for us to reconstruct this topic from a broader, historical perspective. Unlike its predecessors in Norway (1972–1982, 1997–2003), Sweden (1985–1990), and Denmark (1997–2003), VALTA was neither initiated by a government or parliament, nor did it culminate in a report synthesizing its conclusions. It was sponsored by a semi-public research foundation and resembled a thematic multidisciplinary research initiative that called for the implementation of independent projects. It simultaneously placed itself in the tradition of the Scandinavian power investigations and distanced itself from them because of its autonomy and the multiple perspectives embodied in its approach. This counterpoint to the Scandinavian model of public investigation obscures one of its important ideological purposes: providing the public open access to the inner workings of power, and thereby increasing possibilities for participatory democracy, accountability and trust. VALTA has permitted a fresh look back at the results of all power investigations and their role in the public discourse about power. It also reminds us of the continuing relevance of power studies as a unique form of public inquiry in the Nordic countries.

The contributions to this thematic issue were written by academics from the disciplines of history, political science and media and communications studies, all of whom combine an interest in social theory with empirical historical exploration. The introductory article by Norbert Götz gives an overview of the power investigation as a politico-cultural practice that has evolved in the Nordic countries over the past decades. Carl Marklund contextualizes the Swedish investigation in the reconfiguration of the welfare state that took place in the 1980s, arguing that the efforts to renew Swedish public administration led to a discursive change from planning and rationalization to the new language of public service, participation and openness. Ann-Cathrine Jungar takes a comparative perspective on the issue of popular rule and multilevel governance from 1997 to 2003, and shows how public investigations of democracy and power in Denmark, Norway and Sweden, viewed through their narratives about integration into the European Union, national sovereignty and domestic power relations, reveal historically and socially influential differences in experience and outlook.

The two final contributions by Lotta Lounasmeri and Ainur Elmgren provide analyses of the most recent power investigation in Finland from two different viewpoints. From her vantage point as a participant, Lounasmeri discusses some results of the VALTA programme in challenging the existing power structures. Her article provides an endogenous glimpse into the power investigation, expanding the concept to include the societal role of the media. Elmgren offers the first scholarly appraisal of VALTA and its reception as seen by an outsider. Her article explores the contradictory expectations placed on the most recent power investigation, which was different in character and aims from the publicly commissioned Scandinavian investigations, and yet was expected to provide comparable data about Finland and fulfil similar needs in the public discourse.

The idea for this special issue arose within the research project *'Nordic Openness: Opportunities and Limits of a Consensual Political Culture'*, funded by the Network of European Studies at the University of Helsinki and by the Kone Foundation. The contributions exemplify interdisciplinary area studies that examine the concepts and practices that shape the notions of a specific region, in this case the Nordic countries. The authors present a variety of views, including awareness of the affirmative potential of power investigations, their nature as political rather than scholarly projects, their language and their historical and social contexts. The integration of theory and methodology across disciplines shows the potential of area studies and, it is our hope, demonstrates its fruitfulness for the analysis of complex social phenomena.

In addition to the six thematic articles in this issue, we are publishing two additional articles, both of which address the general theme of power, albeit from a distinctive perspective. Alex Prichard, in his article on 'Justice and EU Foreign Policy', examines the particular problematic of European claims to 'an ethical foreign policy'. Using insights taken from virtue ethics, he argues for an approach to evaluating the EU which is based on the idea that justice is relative to the virtues that we pursue in our daily lives, and that these virtues can only be properly understood in relation to the practices through which they are realized and the institutions we build to defend them. Accordingly, he argues that we need to disaggregate the EU's institutions and the practices of key officials and the virtues they promote or defend. Alexandra Hennessy's article on 'Informal Governance and the Eurozone Crisis' focuses on the inadequacies of the EU's political architecture and its policy-making processes in the (unforeseen) circumstance of a fundamental systemic crisis. In the absence of appropriate mechanisms of crisis management, consensus-formation and popular legitimation, the inherited informal hegemonic system under German leadership has found itself wanting, threatening the very survival of the Eurozone project.

As usual, the issue is rounded off with a reviews section, which includes a review article of three books relating to religion and religiosity in contemporary European society, along with a further 15 reviews of publications in the field of European area studies.

Note

[1] Research Programme on Power and Society in Finland, 2007–2010. According to project leader Petteri Pietikäinen (telephone conversation 22 October 2013), the title was selected to avoid the ambiguity of the English word 'power', which also means 'energy'.

Introspective Performance: The Scandinavian Power Investigation as a Politico-Cultural Practice

NORBERT GÖTZ

Södertörn University, Sweden

ABSTRACT   *The transdisciplinary coherence of area studies can be enhanced through a cross-fertilisation of historical and social sciences with concepts derived from philology and cultural studies. The five Scandinavian power investigations (Norway 1972–1982, Sweden 1985–1990, Denmark 1997–2003, Norway 1997–2003, and Finland 2007–2010) are here recognised as a unique body of work. Blending politically guided perspectives with collaborative scholarly analysis, these investigations represent events rather than texts. For this reason the concept of genre does not sufficiently capture their essence. Instead, power investigations are seen as comprehensive politico-cultural practices identified by 14 characteristics imported from the humanities. The utility of these investigations in suggesting transparency and self-reflection enhances the legitimacy of Scandinavian government.*

> Outside of a dog, a book is man's best friend. Inside of a dog it's too dark to read. –
>
> Groucho Marx

The blind confidence that Swedish citizens have in their institutions frequently puzzles foreign observers.[1] In his essay 'Swedish Autumn', Hans Magnus Enzensberger suggested the historical absence of negative experience with political power as a rationale. In a country like Sweden, the 'armed hunting-down of human beings' (Enzensberger 1989, 14) seemed unimaginable. From his German perspective, Enzensberger thought one could only confirm the Swedes in trusting their own system's humanitarianism. Hence, the functionalist concrete-box architecture of the institutions occupying the centres of Swedish towns stood as 'a power that is alien yet always benevolent' (ibid.). This orientation gave moral immunity to the social engineering of society: 'To limit, supervise, and resist the forces of good can only help the forces of evil' (ibid.). Such evidence enabled state authority to expand, permeate remote corners of everyday life, and regulate personal affairs to a degree unparalleled in other Western societies. According to Enzensberger, an observer of Sweden was struck by its genuinely impersonal reason—symbolised by the country's autonomous public administration office, the *ämbetsverk*—which, in a manner of enlightened absolutism, dominated all aspects of Swedish life.

In view of the subtle diffusion of power in its social structures, power issues have traditionally been little discussed in the public sector and academia in Sweden. As political scientist Bernd Henningsen noticed in the mid-1980s, power was not regarded as a problem in its own right; it was seen as simply ingrained in the concept of administration (1986, 367f). However, at about the same time this observation was published, the Swedish government established a scholarly commission of inquiry called a 'power investigation' (*maktutredning*). Its mission was 'to analyse the distribution of power and influence within different sectors of Swedish society' (Maktutredningen 1990, 411).

Henningsen was also the organiser of a conference on a Norwegian power investigation that had operated from 1972 to 1982. His conclusion was reminiscent of Enzensberger's portrait of Sweden in stating that the Norwegian power investigation, with its disregard of personal power and of factors beyond so-called public choice, had 'fallen for the most perfect form of democratic exercise of power: the disguise of power' (Henningsen 1988, 80). Thus, he claimed that the investigation had 'not investigated power at all', but rather accomplished an 'empirical screening of Norwegian society for political and social conditions' (ibid.).

Henningsen's analysis builds on Eric Voegelin's comment that, under the pressure of democratic symbolism, modern political theory has difficulty distinguishing between rulers and subjects—despite the fact that 'ruling power is ruling power even in a democracy' (Voegelin 1952, 38). Nonetheless, Henningsen did acknowledge the discursive reorientation taking place in Scandinavia in the 1970s and 1980s. By including the word 'power' in the standard inventory of scholarly and public debate, an interest was raised calling attention to power as one of the 'old, classical issues of politics' (1988, 75, 82). For Henningsen, even innocuous positivist data-collection under the heading of 'power' activated some of the critical potential inscribed in its conceptual history (see Faber, Ilting, and Meier 1982). The present article unwraps this ambivalence through a generic examination of the characteristics of the Scandinavian power investigations. The historical and social sciences are thereby supplied with concepts derived from philology and cultural studies to suggest ways of integrating the disciplines forming the core of area studies.

'Power Investigations' and Their Antecedents

Studies on the power of government are at least as old as Thucydides' *History of the Peloponnesian War* written in the fifth century BC. On ceremonial occasions the northern European tradition of 'power investigation' is traced back to Snorri Sturluson's *Heimskringla*, a thirteenth-century collection of kings' sagas written in Old Norse (Østerud 1999a, 11). The author was an Icelandic subject of the Norwegian crown who was loyal to the king and on very good terms with the dynasty about which he wrote.

Commissions of inquiry form another part of the background of power investigations. The institution plays a prominent role in Sweden, but it is also a significant feature of Finnish and Norwegian politics (Pedersen and Lægreid 1994, 253–7). Such commissions of inquiry have been at the centre of Scandinavian politics since the nineteenth century. Characteristic is their multi-partite parliamentary composition and the general inclusion of representatives of civil society, organisations and academia (Rainio-Niemi 2010). Also significant is the pragmatic approach of such commissions to problems of society with a social engineering approach (Marklund 2008). The reports of their inquiry are meticulously documented and a major source on Scandinavian societies. The institution has declined over the past two decades (Nybom 2010; Rainio-Niemi 2010), although the power investigations, with their broad mandate extending over several years without any immediate political utility being demanded of them, continue to resemble the commissions of old.

A direct predecessor of the power investigations was the comprehensive Swedish inquiry on emigration to the United States (*Emigrationsutredningen*), carried out at the beginning of the twentieth century under the leadership of statistician Gustav Sundbärg and published in 21 volumes. It identified the discontent of ordinary people who felt 'discomforting powerlessness' before the upper class and their country's strong bureaucracy as a factor driving many Swedes to emigrate (Sundbärg 1913, 840, see also 836).

The first modern power investigation goes back to the programme announced by the Norwegian Labour Party for their first 100 days in office after winning the election of 1969 (Diskussionsbeiträge 1988, 91; statement by G. Hernes). The initiative is ascribed to a labour programme committee that was called 'the think tank' (*tænkeloftet*). Its initial interest was primarily the issue of economic power.[2] It can be seen as a reaction to the western protest movements of 1968. Despite winning the elections, it took the Labour Party a long time to implement their programme: the projected 100 days turned into 1,000 days (Diskussionsbeiträge 1988, 91; statement by G. Hernes). In the end, the power investigation became the last decision of the Labour government before a referendum on membership in the European Communities (which demonstrated the power of the people) triggered the resignation of the government in September 1972 (Hernes 1988, 58).

Sociologist Gudmund Hernes, one of the three leaders of the power investigation, later referred to it as a 'kamikaze mission', for which it was difficult to recruit members and whose feasibility was widely doubted in academia (Diskussionsbeiträge 1988, 91— statement by G. Hernes). The investigation was also led by Johan P. Olsen, a political scientist, and Håvard Alstadheim, an economist, who played a minor role. The government had stated that it was 'of fundamental importance that the actual power relations are unveiled and disclosed for public debate and critical analysis', so the commission was tasked with bringing about 'the best possible knowledge of the real power relations in Norwegian society' (Maktutredningen 1982, 1). The commission submitted its final report in 1982. Altogether, 20 books and approximately 100 working papers were published in its name. The commission saw its mission as that of an empirical inquiry along the lines of the dominant US political science paradigm of quantification. Thus, its leader boasted of having collected approximately 1 million 'single findings' (Hernes 1988, 58). Consider that the inquiry cost 7 million NOK, each finding cost an average of 7 NOK. In addition to the three team leaders, a total of 20 scholars worked on the inquiry for a minimum of half a year, and 12 scholars were given additional research assignments (Maktutredningen 1982, 263f). Despite its modest funding and the objections that might be raised against its positivist orientation, the Norwegian power investigation of the 1970s set a remarkable academic benchmark, demonstrating a higher standard of theory development and research organisation than that of preceding Scandinavian research programmes (Micheletti 1984, 341).

The Swedish power investigation ran from 1985 to 1990 under the leadership of political scientist Olof Petersson, its chairman, along with historian Yvonne Hirdman, and economist Inga Persson. Johan P. Olsen was included in the team as expert member based on his experience with the Norwegian predecessor inquiry. However, Petersson has stated that the Norwegian model's concepts such as the 'iron triangle', 'media-twisted society' or 'segmented state' had greater appeal than its actual empirical research findings. He observed that a research project of its own would be required to determine why a Swedish power investigation was established in the first place. The perceived need of developing a timely self-understanding for a rapidly changing society was probably crucial (Petersson 1988, 146). The official mandate of the commission was to analyse the distribution of power and influence in different sectors of Swedish society, particularly with regard to the constitutive factors of democracy. The Swedish commission published about as much as the Norwegian one, but its budget of 33 million SEK was considerably greater and its number of participants (142 in all) was significantly larger, including a board with James G. March, Fritz W. Scharpf, Theda Skocpol, Sidney Verba and other internationally known academics (Maktutredningen 1990, 411, 421, 437–44).

There have been a number of related commissions of inquiry following the power investigation. Apart from the broadly based 'democracy investigation' (*Demokrati-utredning* in Jungar's contribution to this theme issue this investigation is included in a Scandinavian comparison of power investigations of the late 1990s; Jungar 2013) inquiries on narrower topics have examined women and men in power positions in Swedish society, the power, integration and structural discrimination, and the distribution of economic power and resources between women and men. Once positioned in political discourse, the topic of power became almost omnipresent.

In Denmark, a power investigation was first suggested in 1988 by a socialist member of parliament. However, the proposal did not gain support until 1994, when it was hoped that an investigation would uncover the prevailing disparity of financial resources of interest organisations, on the one hand, and political parties, on the other (Frandsen 2004). Aiming at a greater allocation of public funds to the latter, the Danish parliament established an ad hoc committee for the analysis of democracy and power. In Spring 1997, this committee passed the initiative on to a scholarly commission that

> in the coming years can more systematically explore the essence of discussions and dilemmas of democracy in a modern welfare society as it approaches the threshold of a new century, and also lay bare the channels of power and influence that exist in a society in close contact with global and technological reality.[3]

In May of that year, the government appointed a political scientist, Lise Togeby, as chairwoman. By November, three more political scientists (Jørgen Goul Andersen, Peter Munk Christiansen and Torben Beck Jørgensen), as well as public health scholar Signild Vallgårda, were added to the team. Following the investigation, there was criticism of the commission's lopsided disciplinary composition, particularly the specialisation of its political scientists in the fields of participation and administration, and its alleged systematic disregard of issues related to economic power. The investigation had a budget of 50 million DKK and produced approximately 50 books and 35 other publications until its mandate expired in 2003 (Frandsen 2004).[4]

Almost parallel to the Danish inquiry, a Norwegian 'Power and Democracy Investigation' (*Makt- og demokratiutredning*) was appointed. Its name reflected the explicit focus on the condition and future of the democratic exercise of power that had been established by the Swedish inquiry. The decision to establish a new power investigation was unanimously approved by parliament in October 1996. In December of the following year, its mandate was stated as inquiring into the way 'representative democracy and its prerequisites are challenged and affected' by factors that had not been relevant in the previous investigation. These factors were later specified as marketisation, internationalisation, new technologies, opinion making, environmental challenges, multiculturalism and the knowledge society, in addition to tendencies of decentralisation, citizen participation in government and changing role of voluntary associations. The sum appropriated for this purpose was 49 million NOK (Mandat 1999, 144, 146, 162–3). The group was led by three political scientists—Øyvind Østerud (chairman), Per Selle and Hege Skjeie—sociologist Fredrik Engelstad, and art historian Siri Meyer. Its disciplinary range was not only wider than that of its Danish counterpart, but the Norwegian political scientists also represented a broader spread of interests than their Danish colleagues.

The second Norwegian power investigation produced 52 books, 76 working papers and numerous articles. However, a consensus report by the leadership group was not among its accomplishments. Only the three male members of the group agreed to a joint résumé (Østerud, Engelstad, and Selle 2003). An official final report was also published, to which Skjeie and Meyer contributed dissenting statements. Skjeie criticised the disregard of gender imbalances as well as thinking in the category of the nation-state, saying it turned the external world into a threat rather than an opportunity. Meyer's objection was directed at what she perceived as her colleagues' formalistic, inhuman and instrumental concept of power; she proposed an alternative, culturalist understanding of the political (Makt- og demokratiutredningen 2003). By the time the final report appeared, she had already resigned from the commission and published her own unofficial conclusions under the title *The Empire Calls* (*Imperiet kaller*; Meyer 2003).

The divergent tendency of the two investigations that were active in the years 1997–2003 is striking. Despite disagreements within the Norwegian steering committee, its members generally had a pessimistic and critical perspective on the condition of their country's democratic system. According to the majority opinion, Norway's institutions were in a state of gradual decline. By contrast, the Danish commission concluded, 'It has actually gone astonishingly well. There is still democratic vigour in the Danish population and considerable democratic robustness in its political institutions. Above all, the Danish population seems both resourceful and capable of action' (Togeby et al. 2003, 402).

There has not been a state-run power investigation in Finland. However, in the 1970s there was a research programme dealing with equality and democracy called TANDEM (*Tasa-arvon ja demokratian tutkimus*) that worked on similar issues from a Marxist point of view and is today considered a reference programme (Tasa-arvon ja demokratiantutki-mus 1977). In 2004 the Westermarck Society, a Finnish sociological association, requested that the Academy of Finland initiate a research programme on the country's power system. Despite the fact that the Academy's call for proposals quoted the sociologists' memorandum word for word in parts, only two sociology projects received research grants. The main emphasis among the 24 projects receiving funding for the period 2007–2010 (sharing a total budget of 6.5 million Euros) was on political science, economics and social psychology. The sociologists had pointed to the Scandinavian power

Table 1. Overview over power investigations

	Norway	Sweden	Denmark	Finland	Iceland/Scandinavia
ca. 1225					*Heimskringla*
1913		*Emigrationsutredningen: Betänkande i utvandringsfrågan*			
1977				TANDEM: *Demokratian rajat ja rakenteet*	
1982	**Maktutredningen: Sluttrapport**				
1990		**Demokrati och makt i Sverige: Maktutredningens huvudrapport**			
2003	**Makt og demokrati: Sluttrapport fra Maktog demokratiutredningen**		*Togeby et al.: Magt og demokrati i Danmark. Hovedresultater fra Magtudredningen.*		
2005				**Petteri Pietikäinen (ed.): Valta Suomessa**	
2010					*Demokrati i Norden*

Other classic studies of power
Arendt, H. 1970. *On Violence*. New York: Harcourt, Brace & World.
Castells, M. 2009. *Communication Power*. Oxford: Oxford University Press.
Enquete-Kommission 'Aufarbeitung von Geschichte und Folgen der SED-Diktatur in Deutschland' 1995. *Materialien*. Baden-Baden: Nomos.
Foucault, M. 1961. *Folie et Déraison*. Paris: Union Générale d'Éditions.
Gramsci, A. 1948–1951. *Quaderni dal Carcere*. Turin: Einaudi.
Machiavelli, N. 1532. *Il Principe*. Florence: Giunta.
de Montesquieu, Ch. 1748. *De L'esprit des Loix*. Geneva: Barrillot.
Rhodes, R. A. W. 2000. *Transforming British Government*, vols 1–2 [the so-called Whitehall Programme]. Basingstoke: Macmillan.
Thucydides. 1900 [5th century bc]. *History of the Peloponnesian War*. Oxford: Clarendon.
de Tocqueville, A. 1835–1840. *La Démocratie en Amérique*, vols 1–2 Paris: Gosselin.

investigations as models for a Finnish programme, underlining their pragmatic approach based in organisation theory and their interest in issues concerning democracy and administration.[5] In referring extensively to the Scandinavian power investigations in their call for proposals, the Finnish Academy made it clear that they intended their research programme as the functional equivalent. In studying the complex processes of the allocation of power, the Academy claimed, Finland would join (*liittää*) the 'Nordic studies on power, but it also produces new knowledge on the specific characteristics and historical differences of Finnish power structures as compared to those of the other Nordic countries' (Suomen Akatemia 2005, 53, see also 8, 51–2).[6]

Iceland is the only Scandinavian country that has not yet had a comprehensive research programme on power. However, in 2004 the Icelandic government initiated a study on the state of democracy within the framework of Nordic cooperation that was in particular based on the Danish and the second Norwegian power investigations. Fredrik Engelstad, a former leader of the Norwegian research group was one of the co-authors of this study (Demokratiudvalget 2005).

Table 1 provides an overview of power studies in Scandinavia and includes other classic studies of power. The emboldened areas indicate those 'power investigations' that are the focus of this article.

The 'Power Investigation' as a Politico-Cultural Practice

Power investigations are a form of collective action enacted in a ritual manner particular to the Scandinavian type of 'open society' (see Petersson 1989). They are cathartic performances of self-enlightenment and self-assurance. Thus, the power investigations are part of the problem they purport to analyse. A humanistic framework of analysis makes visible the hidden agenda of the power investigations and identifies them in their larger societal context. The criteria for this study were derived inductively in the course of the analysis of power investigations. A comment by the chairman of the second Norwegian inquiry, Øyvind Østerud, who characterised power investigations as a genre that had specific qualities and shortcomings, provided a good starting point:

> There is a limitation with regard to the power investigation as a genre. It provides a research topic; it can describe the development of power structures as a historical 'education novel' [*dannelsesfortelling*], or it can chart the aspects and mechanisms of power as a contemporary 'digression novel' [*digresjonsroman*]. But it does not have the revealing intention of the detective story or investigation. With regard to individual matters and the concrete decision making process, a more generalising power investigation will not be able to name particular power holders and power structures. Here, research takes a different vantage point than both an investigation and investigative journalism. This limits the concrete respect in which a research programme can say something new and unexpected, since the programme aims at the more general traits in the transformation of power and the conditions of popular government. (Østerud 1999a, 16)

In considering the limitations of 'power investigation' as a genre, approaches advocating genres as social action point in the right direction (Miller 1984). But the various generic typologies of different disciplines are insufficient if we attempt to apply them to an analysis of Scandinavian power investigations.

At the end of the eighteenth century, Wilhelm von Humboldt (1963, 153) expressed the conviction that there was no field of human activity in which it was possible to achieve utmost perfection outside the boundaries of that genre. A few years later it became the goal of Romanticism to transcend the limits of genres. In the complex world of today, the challenge is to transcend the limits of the text-centred notion of genre by engaging in transdisciplinary research. The process-oriented and holistic concept of 'politico-cultural practice' employed in the present analysis builds on existing taxonomic approaches, but applies a broader perspective. In particular it uses ideas imported from speech act theory, communication-oriented text linguistics, sociological poetics and reader-response criticism (Bakhtin 1981a; Brinker et al. 2000; Jauss 1982; Searle 1969; Tompkins 1980). It combines elements of the above in attempting a comprehensive study of power investigations. Not only are those investigations taken as producers of societal analyses— they are understood as social events in their own right.

This concurs with topical research that prefers multilevel models to characterise text types and genres. These are thought of as historically variable and culturally conditioned entities that are constantly challenged and modified by new works (Heinemann and Heinemann 2002). The analytical tool of politico-cultural practice establishes a plausible level of abstraction for complex phenomena such as power investigations, while still exhibiting parallels to familiar concepts.

The following 14-point overview moves from textual variables to contextual ones. It presents preliminary findings and hypotheses, based on a reading of the final reports of the various inquiries and other documents, and assesses the degree to which the investigations correspond to the ideal type of the power investigation as a politico-cultural practice.[7] The intention here goes beyond the empirical analysis, to suggesting an analytical framework derived from philology and cultural studies for historical and social science purposes in a regional context. The goal is to consolidate area studies by means of a transdisciplinary integration of theory and methodology using a concrete Scandinavian example.

The characteristics and their properties considered representative for the politico-cultural practice 'power investigation' are as follows.

1. Power investigations are characterised by the *discourse* in which they partake. By their designation and raison d'être, all programmes locate themselves firmly in the discourse about power.
2. *Intertextuality*, the reference to or self-declaration as a power-investigation, is a second characteristic. Evidently, this criterion cannot be meaningfully applied to the Norwegian power investigation that invented the politico-cultural practice. All other power investigations place themselves in the tradition thereby established—usually by their naming, but otherwise also by reference to the previous inquiries in programmatic documents.
3. The *chronotope*, the space–time matrix inherent in human thought, is a concept from physics which has been introduced to literary studies by Mikhail M. Bakhtin (1981b). The chronotope characteristic of the power investigations is the 'grand narrative' of an a-historical nation state with welfare state quality. The tendency of the last inquiries, postulating a more or less successful

resistance to historically contingent impositions of globalisation and post-modernisation, pronounces this frame of reference particularly.

4. In regard to the characteristic *register* or language code of the power investigations, the Swedish term 'inquiry prose' (*utredningsprosa*) is helpful. It signifies a hybrid diction consisting of bureaucratic formulae, legal hedging, scholarly abstraction, and political correctness. The point made here would benefit from detailed comparative studies on the use of language. As to the Finnish programme, a more scholarly style can be assumed because of the more clear-cut academic background of this inquiry. However, by definition there is a considerable overlap of 'inquiry prose' and mainstream scholarly writing.

5. An *initiator* is significant for any politico-cultural practice. In the case of the last power investigation, this was the Academy of Finland, a semi-governmental research funding agency. However, power investigations have typically been appointed by governments or parliaments. The fact that the first two power investigations were convened by governments, while the two that followed were called by parliaments might be a result of the increasingly perceived 'democracy deficit' of modern interdependent statehood. As the foremost representatives of the power of the sovereign people, legislators might feel that their influence has been waning in the past decades.

6. Post-structural literary theory has proclaimed the death of the author, meaning that the monopoly of interpretation from an author's perspective is obsolete (Barthes 1967). Similarly, from a linguistic point of view, the emitter of a message has lost authority. In the framework of politico-cultural practice, the corresponding concept would be that of the *performer*. Power investigations are much more than occasions for producing documents: they are rituals of societal self-absorption and a search for meaning. A common trait of the performers of power investigations, whether living or dead, is that they all come from academia.

7. The *generation* of the power investigation analyses is done by multiple scholarly voices and numerous publications. In the case of the Finnish programme, the final anthology speaks of 'a polyphonic collage, not in lock-step, but different variations on a basic theme: power in Finland' (Pietikäinen 2010b, 10). The other investigations were also based on multiple perspectives. To what degree such polyphony is orchestrated and characterised by consonance or dissonance is a question that has no simple answer.

8. The politico-cultural practice of 'power investigation' features a sequential-hierarchic *staging* dramaturgy whose final report is the authoritative pooling of a small steering group, usually consisting of three to five scholars. Even the second Norwegian commission followed this pattern, despite the fact that no synthesis was achieved because of irreconcilable differences within the leadership circle. The Finnish programme, which consisted of 24 autonomous projects that did not rely on an overall academic leadership, nevertheless culminated in a final publication in which approximately half of the projects presented themselves individually. The Finnish volume also contains an introductory and concluding essay by programme manager Petteri Pietikäinen, who was employed by the Academy of Finland. The selection of the projects to be included was made by the publisher together with the programme manager and based on how well the contributions fitted one of three main topics: history,

legitimacy and people's power (Pietikäinen 2010a). In addition, the Finnish programme produced a final internal report, in which all projects summarised their findings individually (Pietikäinen 2010c), held a final seminar in September 2011, and an evaluation seminar in April 2012.

9. With regard to the *function* of the power investigations, Eckard Rolf's taxonomy of functional text types is helpful, although for the present context these have to be thought of in a broader sense as politico-cultural practices (Rolf 1993). Analogous to Rolf's classification, the societal introspection of power investigations can be classed as 'assertive-descriptive' (*assertiv-registrierend*), that is, as 'noting facts'. For example, the mandate of the first Norwegian commission cautioned members that they should by no means succumb to the temptation of submitting suggestions for a change of power relations (Maktutredningen 1982, 1). This cautious approach was internalised by successor inquiries.

10. The *validity claim* of the investigations discussed here is that of a synthesised truth (see Klein 2000). This suggests an entanglement of the truth claim of classical science with the procedural sequence of the power investigations. However, in two cases this can only be applied with reservation. The second Norwegian inquiry aspired to find out the truth, but was subverted by the dissenting opinions of two members in the leadership group. The Finnish final anthology is a collection of individual contributions and that leaves the synopsis to the reader, despite the pre-selection of contributions, and the introductory and concluding essays. Nonetheless, even the Finnish programme aimed for 'a comprehensive interpretation' (Suomen Akatemia 2005, 54, see also 55), although on the basis of a variety of individual perspectives.

11. The *addressee* of power investigations is always the citizenry of the nation. Even in Finland this point was strongly emphasised in the conversation with the programme manager. In the Finnish project anthology, scholars immediately used the rhetoric figure of a national 'we' (Haapala 2010, 23, 24, 26, 32, 33). At the same time, Finnish background documents raise a different claim and give priority to intra-academic goals. From this perspective, the major aims were research excellence and the creation of scholarly networks, especially international ones. There seems to be a discrepancy between how a research funding institution articulates its objectives, on the one hand, and how the people involved think and write, on the other.

12. Power investigations are characterised by their *intermediality*: they are long-term multimedia events. The book form was favoured by all the inquiries, but accompanied by different workshops, discussion meetings, exhibitions, websites, newsletters and films. The plan to organise a rock concert on the topic of 'power and youth' in the framework of the Finnish programme never was realised. The Norwegian final report of 2003 carefully records the press coverage of different phases of the project. The different media refer to one another. The content-related implication of the media change would need to be extracted in detail for a deeper discussion of this point.

13. The dimension of intermediality can be supplemented by asking for the *dominant medium*, that is, the core medium as an independent characteristic. The institution of the power investigation as such can be regarded as such a

Table 2. Conformity with the politico-cultural practice 'power investigation'

Characteristic	Property	Norway 1982	Sweden 1990	Denmark 2003	Norway 2003	Finland 2010
Discourse	Power	+	+	+	+	+
Intertextuality	Explicit reference to the system	N/A	+	+	+	+
Chronotope	Modern welfare state	+	+	+	+	+
Register	'Inquiry prose' (*utredningsprosa*)	+	+	+	+	?
Initiator	State	+	+	+	+	?
Performer	Scholars	+	+	+	+	+
Generation	Polyphone	+	+	+	+	+
Staging	Sequential-hierarchic	+	+	+	+	+
Function	Assertive-descriptive	+	+	+	+	+
Validity claim	Synthesised truth	+	+	+	?	?
Addressee	National public	+	+	+	+	+
Intermediality	Multimedia long-term event	+	+	+	+	+
Dominant media	Institution	+	+	+	+	?
Meta-function	Legitimisation	+	+	+	+	+

medium. Ultimately, the technicist and essentialist understanding of media which is also common in cultural studies obscures insight in alternative ways of sustainable societal communications—as, for example, through performative acts such as the temporary institutionalisation of a power investigation. This perspective concurs with Niklas Luhmann's functionalist concept of media, according to which everything that is used and brought into form as a medium necessarily becomes a medium (Khurana 2004). Hence, media are highly variable semaphore. The installation of a power investigation sends a strong signal that the officials commissioning it regard themselves as possessing legitimate power. The Finnish programme is again somewhat different, as it lacks the institutional core of a group of leading scholars that has characterised the inquiries of its Scandinavian neighbours.

14. Finally, the *meta-function* of power investigations is simply the legitimisation of prevailing domestic conditions. Not only is a 'power investigation' its own dominant medium, it also functions as its own essential message (see McLuhan 1964, 7). An article written by the chairman of the last Norwegian inquiry, Øyvind Østerud, in the country's leading newspaper may serve as an example. Østerud mused that it would be difficult to imagine Italian politicians commissioning a power investigation, communicating that—in contrast to certain other governments—the Scandinavian powers need not shun the penetrating light of scholarly inquiry (Østerud 1999b). Self-investigation makes them a priori appear as good or already reformed. For Scandinavians, power investigations represent an openness and readiness for immanent critique that highlights moral superiority over the rest of the world (see Kettunen 1997, 162 ff.). In this respect, it will be interesting to compare the results of the more conventionally academic Finnish power programme in greater detail. Whereas the Finnish programme description—maybe owing to such a description's function of listing references rather than criticising them—uncritically referred to the Scandinavian power studies, the programme manager and one of the project leaders claimed in personal conversations that at least some of the Finnish researchers were eager to demonstrate to their Scandinavian neighbours what more critical power studies can accomplish. Had this been the overall approach, it would have widened the scope of the politico-cultural practice 'power investigation', if not transformed it. Yet, Finnish academia is traditionally close to the state, and the final project anthology gives little evidence of a more critical attitude as compared to the Scandinavian predecessors (the concluding essay en passant addresses the problem of commissioned research and lack of power of individual researchers to determine their own research topics, though; Pietikäinen 2010d). The proposition of one of the Finnish power researchers, 'Looking through the eyes of nineteenth-century man we now live in the country that utopian socialists dreamed of, though it is capitalist', entails an uplifting empowerment hypothesis. While not representative of the Finnish programme as a whole, it provides a good indication of the general direction (Haapala 2010, 23).

Table 2 summarises the preceding discussion, listing the characteristics and properties of the politico-cultural practice of 'power investigation' as established in the Scandinavian countries. The table also presents preliminary findings on the various cases, based on published final reports and ancillary materials. The degree to which the different investigations correspond to the ideal type of the politico-cultural practice 'power investigation' is indicated by the following symbols: + stands for the criteria having been fully met, and ~ for partial conformity.

Outlook

Society and politics are not only crude spheres of interest maximisation; they can also be seen as symbolic systems and culturally determined patterns for action. The concept 'politico-cultural practice' suggests such a perspective. Its usefulness has been demonstrated by discussing 14 characteristic dimensions of the power investigations that have operated in the Scandinavian countries since the 1970s. At the same time, the analytical framework used here provides an example of how the transdisciplinary coherence of area studies can be enhanced through a cross-fertilisation of historical and social sciences with concepts derived from philology and cultural studies.

Power investigations are examples of the amalgamation of different societal functions and the political instrumentalisation of scholars in the Scandinavian countries. They resemble the practice of auditors being beholden to the companies they are supposed to monitor. The question of how much openness and independence is actually realised in the power investigations could be decisive for the continuation of this politico-cultural practice (Petersson 2003). The recent Finnish experiences might be of particular significance in this respect. Calls for the next power investigation are already being raised in Sweden (Bjereld 2010).

The second Norwegian investigation suggests that a combination of different insights might lead to perspectives for meaningful action. In one paper, the classicist and philosopher Amund Børdahl characterised non-fiction and trivial literature as belonging to the same genre, namely 'power prose' (Børdahl 2003, 48).[8] By contrast he consigns belles-lettres and collections of essays to the sphere of 'impotent prose'. The same author has also suggested a radically formalised power theory along the lines of hardcore US political science, which he derived from the frame of reference of Gudmund Hernes and the first Norwegian power investigation. In its most condensed form, the theory appears as follows:

$$M_p = \sum_s \sum_p m_p l_{ps} k_{ps}$$

This is a nonsense-formula claiming that the power of an author is a function of the interest paid to him or her by other authors (Børdahl 2003, 52)!

Combining the power perspective on the type of prose with that on the author, the challenge of making society a place with a more equitable distribution of power is raising the stakes for those writing 'impotent prose' to such high a level that 'power prose' has to yield. Whether the alternatives really are that clearly demarcated is debatable. The notion that those qualified to act as a corrective to the abuse of power are powerless is distressing. A lack of entanglement in the power structure of a particular country or region might suffice to ensure the critical perspectives demanded; scholarly autonomy is easier developed at a distance than in whatever kind of dependence. The Scandinavian countries, which gave the term 'ombudsman', deserve spokespersons who are not embroiled in their own nation's power structures. Like for any society, such voices are to be found abroad. This is why we need area studies and interaction with foreign observers. Even in the democratic polities of today, societal analysis is too precious to be left to the 'prince' and his domestic scholarly henchmen.

Notes

[1] This article is part of the project *'Nordic Openness: Opportunities and Limits of a Consensual Political Culture'*, funded by the Network for European Studies at the University of Helsinki and the Kone Foundation. I am indebted to Ainur Elmgren for her help with Finnish source material. An earlier version has been published in German as Götz (2010).

[2] http://webarkiv.ft.dk/?/Samling/19951/udvbilag/UDM/Almdel_bilag10.htm, http://webarkiv.ft.dk/?/Samling/19951/udvbilag/UDM/Almdel_bilag11.htm.

[3] Beretning afgivet af Udvalget vedrørende analyse af demokrati og magt i Danmark den 19. marts 1997 [Report of the committee on the analysis of democracy and power in Denmark, 19 March 1997], available at: http://webarkiv.ft.dk/?/Samling/19961/udvbilag/UDM/Almdel_bilag23.htm.

[4] The final report is in Togeby et al. (2003).

[5] Suomalainen valtajärjestelmä. Muistio 30.4.2004 [The Finnish power system: Memorandum, 30 April 2004]. (This is the memorandum by the Westermarck Society, private copy.)

[6] This statement can be seen in a general context of Nordic/Scandinavian tradition and orientation in Finland (Erkkilä 2010).

[7] For the Finnish power investigation, a programme anthology (Pietikäinen 2010a, 2010b) was used, in addition to a call for proposals from 2005 and two interviews with the programme coordinator, Petteri Pietikäinen (January 2008 and January 2010).

[8] Perspectives for future power research may especially be found in studies about power over language and concepts, such as Kananen and Kantola (2009).

References

Arendt, H. 1970. *On Violence*. New York: Harcourt, Brace & World.

Bakhtin, M. M. 1981a. *The Dialogic Imagination*. Austin: University of Texas Press.

Bakhtin, M. M. 1981b. "Forms of Time and of the Chronotope in the Novel." In *The Dialogic Imagination*, 84–258. Austin: University of Texas Press.

Barthes, R. 1967. "The Death of the Author." *Aspen* (5–6): n.p.

Bjereld, U. 2010. "Makten att skapa makt." [The power to mould power] *Dagens Nyheter* (20 January).

Børdahl, A. 2003. "Maktprosa." [Power prose]. In *Maktens Tekster* [Texts of Power], edited by K. L. Berge, S. Meyer, and T. A. Trippestad, 42–61. Oslo: Gyldendal.

Brinker, K., G. Antos, W. Heinemann, and S. F. Sager, eds. 2000. *Linguistics of Text and Conversation: An International Handbook of Contemporary Research*, et al. Berlin: de Gruyter.

Castells, M. 2009. *Communication Power*. Oxford: University Press.

Demokratiudvalget. 2005. *Demokrati i Norden* [Democracy in Scandinavia]. Copenhagen: Nordic Council of Ministers.

Diskussionsbeiträge. 1988. *Norwegische Politikaspekte: Ein Seminarbericht zu außen- und innenpolitischen Fragen in den Achtzigern* [Aspects of Norwegian politics: A seminar report on foreign policy and domestic issues in the eighties], edited by B. Henningsen, 83–93. Baden-Baden: Nomos.

Enquete-Kommission 'Aufarbeitung von Geschichte und Folgen der SED-Diktatur in Deutschland'. 1995. *Materialien*. Baden-Baden: Nomos.

Enzensberger, H. M. 1989. "Swedish Autumn." In *Europe, Europe: Forays into a Continent*, 3–35. London: Hutchinson Radius.

Erkkilä, T. 2010. *Reinventing Nordic Openness: Transparency and State Information in Finland*. Helsinki: University.

Faber, K.-G., K.-H. Ilting, and C. Meier. 1982. "Macht, Gewalt." [Power, Violence] In *Geschichtliche Grundbegriffe: Historisches Lexikon zur politisch-sozialen Sprache in Deutschland, Vol. 3: H–Me*

[Historical key concepts: Historical encyclopedia on the political and social terminology in Germany], edited by O. Brunner, W. Conze, and R. Koselleck, 817–935. Stuttgart: Klett-Cotta.

Foucault, M. 1961. *Folie et Déraison* [Madness and Civilization]. Paris: Union Générale d'Éditions.

Frandsen, A. 2004. "Magtudredningens tilblivelse 1994–1997." [The emergence of the power investigation 1994–1997] In *Magt.dk: Kritik af Magtudredningen* [Power.dk: A critique of the power investigation], edited by J. Øllgaard, and M. O. Madsen, 11–18. Copenhagen: Frydenlund.

Götz, N. 2010. ""Machtuntersuchung" als Selbstaufklärung: Merkmale einer Kulturpraktik." [Power investigation as self-enlightenment: Characteristics of a cultural practice] In *Vom alten Norden zum neuen Europa: Politische Kultur in der Ostseeregion* [From old Norden to the new Europe: Political Culture in the Baltic Sea Region], edited by N. Götz, J. Hecker-Stampehl, and S. M. Schröder, 131–150. Berlin: Wissenschafts-Verlag.

Gramsci, A. 1948–1951. *Quaderni dal Carcere* [Prison Notebooks]. Turin: Einaudi.

Haapala, P. 2010. "Vallan rakenteet ja yteiskunnan muutos: Mielikuvaharjoitus 1800–2000-lukujen Suomesta." [Structures of power and societal change: An exercise in images from 19th and 20th century Finland] In *Valta Suomessa* [Power in Finland], edited by P. Pietikäinen, 21–33. Helsinki: Gaudeamus.

Heinemann, M., and W. Heinemann. 2002. *Grundlagen der Textlinguistik: Interaktion – Text – Diskurs* [Foundations of the linguistics of text: Interaction – text – discourse]. Tübingen: Niemeyer.

Henningsen, B. 1986. *Der Wohlfahrtsstaat Schweden* [The Swedish welfare state]. Baden-Baden: Nomos.

Henningsen, B. 1988. "'Macht' zwischen Wissenschaft und Politik: Kommentar zu Gudmund Hernes." ['Power' between science and politics: Comment on Gudmund Hernes] In *Norwegische Politikaspekte: Ein Seminarbericht zu außen- und innenpolitischen Fragen in den Achtzigern* [Aspects of Norwegian politics: A seminar report on foreign policy and domestic issues in the eighties], edited by B. Henningsen, 73–82. Baden-Baden: Nomos.

Hernes, G. 1988. "Wer regiert die Regierenden? Die norwegische "Machtuntersuchung." [Who governs the governing? The Norwegian 'power investigation'] In *Norwegische Politikaspekte: Ein Seminarbericht zu außen- und innenpolitischen Fragen in den Achtzigern* [Aspects of Norwegian politics: A seminar report on foreign policy and domestic issues in the eighties], edited by B. Henningsen, 57–72. Baden-Baden: Nomos.

Humboldt, W. von. 1963. "Ueber Göthes Herrmann und Dorothea." [About Herrmann and Dorothea by Goethe] In *Werke in fünf Bänden* [Works in five volumes]. Vol. 2, 125–356. Darmstadt: Wissenschaftliche Buchgesellschaft.

Jauss, H. R. 1982. *Toward an Aesthetic of Reception*. Minneapolis: University of Minnesota Press.

Jungar, Ann-Cathrine. 2013. "Three Nordic Power Investigations on the Repercussions of the European Union on Sovereignty and Democracy." *Journal of Contemporary European Studies* 21 (3): 373–382.

Kananen, J., and A. Kantola. 2009. "Kilpailukyky ja tuottavuus: Kuinka uudet käsitteet saavuttivat hallitsevan aseman hyvinvointivaltion muutoksessa." [Competitivity and productivity: How new concepts gained a dominant position in the changing welfare state] In *Ajatuksen voima: Ideat hyvinvointivaltion uudistamisessa* [The power of thought: ideas in the renewal of the welfare state], edited by J. Kananen, and J. Saari, 119–151. Jyväskylä: Sophi/Minerva.

Kettunen, P. 1997. "The Society of Virtuous Circles." In *Models, Modernity and the Myrdals*, edited by P. Kettunen, and H. Eskola, 153–173. Helsinki: University.

Khurana, T. 2004. "Niklas Luhmann: Die Form des Mediums." [Niklas Luhmann: The form of the medium] In *Medientheorien: Eine Philosophische Einführung* [Media theories: A philosophical introduction], edited by A. Lagaay, and D. Lauer, 97–125. Frankfurt am Main: Campus.

Klein, J. 2000. "Intertextualität, Geltungsmodus, Texthandlungsmuster: Drei vernachlässigte Kategorien der Textsortenforschung – exemplifiziert an politischen und medialen Textsorten." [Intertextuality, validity modus, text plot patterns: Three neglected categories of research on textual classes – exemplified with political and media texts] In *Textsorten: Reflexionen und Analysen* [Text classes: Reflections and analyses], edited by K. Adamzik, 31–44. Tübingen: Stauffenburg.

Machiavelli, N. 1532. *Il Principe* [The prince]. Florence: Giunta.

Makt- og demokratiutredningen. 2003. *Makt og demokrati: Sluttrapport fra Makt- og demokratiutredningen* [Democracy and power in Sweden: Final report of the power investigation]. Oslo: Statens Forvaltningstjeneste.

Maktutredningen. 1982. *Maktutredningen: Sluttrapport*. Oslo: Universitetsforlaget.

Maktutredningen. 1990. *Demokrati och makt i Sverige: Maktutredningens huvudrapport*. Stockholm: Allmänna.

Mandat for en utredning om makt og demokrati [Mandate for an investigation on power and democracy]. 1999. *Mot en ny maktutredning* [Towards a new power investigation], edited by Ø. Østerud, et al., 144–164. Oslo: Gyldendal.

Marklund, C. 2008. *Bridging Politics and Science: The Concept of Social Engineering in Sweden and the USA, Circa 1890–1950.* Florence: European University Institute.

McLuhan, M. 1964. *Understanding media: The Extensions of Man.* New York: McGraw-Hill.

Meyer, S. 2003. *Imperiet kaller: Et essay om maktens anatom* [The empire calls: An essay on the anatomy of power]. Oslo: Spartacus.

Micheletti, M., J. P. Olsen, H. Saetren, G. Hernes, W. Martinussen, E. Damgaard, J. Westerstahl, and F. Johansson. 1984. "Democracy and Political Power in Denmark, Norway and Sweden: A Review-essay." *Western Political Quarterly* 37 (2): 324–342.

Miller, C. R. 1984. "Genre as Social Action." *Quarterly Journal of Speech* 70 (2): 151–167.

Montesquieu, Ch. de. 1748. *De L'esprit des Loix* [The spirit of the laws]. Geneva: Barrillot.

Nybom, T. 2010. "Politik, Wissen, Macht und Gesellschaft: Sehr persönliche Überlegungen zu einem weberianischen Thema [Politics, knowledge, power, and society: Personal reflections on a Weberian theme]." In *Vom alten Norden zum neuen Europa: Politische Kultur in der Ostseeregion*, edited by N. Götz, J. Hecker-Stampehl, and S. M. Schröder, 391–408. Berlin: Wissenschafts-Verlag.

Østerud, Ø. 1999a. "Folkets veje i dansk politik." [The people's path into Danish politics] In *Mot en ny maktutredning* [Towards a new power investigation], edited by Ø. Østerud, et al., 11–18. Oslo: Gyldendal.

Østerud, Ø. 1999b. "Makt og avmakt." [Power and powerlessness] *Aftenposten* (8 November).

Østerud, Ø., F. Engelstad, and P. Selle. 2003. [Power and democracy: A final book from the investigation on power and democracy]. Oslo: Gyldendal.

Pedersen, O. K., and P. Lægreid. 1994. "Maktutredningen slutrapport (nou 1982: 3)." [The final report of the power investigation (nou 1982: 3)] In *Forvaltningspolitik i Norden* [Administration policy in Scandinavia], edited by P. Lægreid, and O. K. Pedersen, 249–281. Copenhagen: Jurist- og økonomforbundet.

Petersson, O. 1988. "The Study of Power and Democracy in Sweden." *Scandinavian Political Studies* 11 (2): 145–158.

Petersson, O. 1989. *Makt i det öppna samhället* [Power in the open society]. Stockholm: Carlsson.

Petersson, O. 2003. "Den sista maktutredningen?" *Nytt Norsk Tidsskrift* [The last power investigation?] (20):351–362.

Pietikäinen, P., ed. 2010a. *Valta Suomessa* [Power in Finland]. Helsinki: Gaudeamus.

Pietikäinen, P. 2010b. "Johdanto: Epäilyttävä, houkutteleva valta." [Introduction: Suspicious, enticing power]. In *Valta Suomessa*, 7–18. Helsinki: Gaudeamus.

Pietikäinen, P., ed. 2010c. *Valta-ohjelmanhankkeiden tulokset* [Results of the projects of the Valta programme]. Helsinki: Academy of Finland.

Pietikäinen, P. 2010d. "Lopuksi: Kansalaiset valtaa vahtimassa." [Conclusion: Citizens monitoring power]. In *Valta Suomessa*, edited by P. Pietikäinen, 251–259. Helsinki: Gaudeamus.

Rainio-Niemi, J. 2010. "State Committees in Finland in Historical Comparative Perspective." In *Nordic associations in a European perspective*, edited by R. Alapuro, and Henrik Stenius, 241–268. Baden-Baden: Nomos.

Rhodes, R. A. W. 2000. *Transforming British Government*. Vols 1–2. Basingstoke: Macmillan.

Rolf, E. 1993. *Die Funktionen der Gebrauchstextsorten* [The functions of utility text types]. Berlin: de Gruyter.

Searle, J. R. 1969. *Speech Acts: An essay in the Philosophy of Language*. Cambridge: University Press.

Sundbärg, G. 1913. *Emigrationsutredningen: Betänkande i utvandringsfrågan och därmed sammanhängande spörsmål* [The emigration inquiry: Report on the emigration issue and related questions]. Stockholm: Norstedt.

Suomen Akatemia. 2005. *Valta Suomessa (VALTA) 2007–2010 -tutkimusohjelma: Ohjelmamuistio* [Research programme on power in Finland (VALTA) 2007–2010: Programme memorandum]. Helsinki: Suomen Akatemia.

Tasa-arvon ja demokratiantutkimus, ed. 1977. *Demokratian rajat ja rakenteet: Tutkimus suomalaisesta hallitsemistavasta ja sen taloudellisesta perustasta* [Limits and structures of democracy: An investigation in the Finnish method of governance and its economic foundation]. Porvoo: Söderström.

Thucydides. 1900. *History of the Peloponnesian War*. Oxford: Clarendon.

Tocqueville, A. de. 1835–1840. *La Démocratie en Amérique* [Democracy in America]. Vols 1–2. Paris: Gosselin.

Togeby, L., J. G. Andersen, P. M. Christiansen, T. B. Jørgensen, and S. Vallgårda 2003. *Magt og demokrati i Danmark: Hovedresultater fra Magtudredningen* [Power and democracy in Denmark: Main results of the power investigation]. Aarhus: Universitetsforlag.

Tompkins, J. P., ed. 1980. *Reader-response Criticism: From Formalism to Post-structuralism*. Baltimore: John Hopkins University Press.

Voegelin, E. 1952. *The New Science of Politics: An Introduction*. Chicago: University Press.

From the Swedish Model to the Open Society: The Swedish Power Investigation and the Power to Investigate Power, 1985–1990

CARL MARKLUND

Södertörn University, Huddinge, Sweden

ABSTRACT *This article analyses the background, activities and reception of the Swedish power investigation (1985–1990). It argues that the power investigation had to navigate between two distinct expectations: on the one hand, the investigation was to expose private power in the interest of equality and justice; on the other hand, it was to improve the exercise of public power in the interest of democracy and efficiency. Because of this two-fold objective, the power investigation was criticised for having neither disclosed private power openly enough, nor pointed out possible ways of adequately rejuvenating welfare state policies clearly. However, the article concludes that one may also assess the power investigation insofar as it served to reconceptualise the socio-political language of welfare state politics in general, as a result of the power inherent in the right to investigate power.*

After decades of continuous economic growth and ambitious social reforms, the Swedish welfare state came under increasing criticism in the 1970s for being bureaucratic, inefficient and even undemocratic. Much of this criticism, voiced from the left and the right, as well as from the emerging environmental movement, focused upon the supposedly corporatist elements of the Swedish welfare state model (Ehnmark and Enquist 1987; Frenander 1998; Mellbourn 1986; Wiklund 2006).

More specifically, however, the criticism turned against the alleged hegemony of the Swedish Social Democratic Workers' Party (*Sveriges socialdemokratiska arbetareparti*; SAP) as the main architect of the welfare state. Social democracy was being accused of having become too powerful during its long period in office (1932–1976). Leading social democrats, by contrast, perceived themselves as less powerful than before, feeling themselves increasingly tied down by both the external pressures of the world economy as well as the internal power structures of the corporatist and increasingly complex Swedish welfare state model itself.

Several political scientists agreed with this characterisation, concluding that the traditional 'independence' of Swedish authorities from direct governmental influence had made it more difficult to exercise political power (Mellbourn 1986; Tarschys 1978). The incoming bourgeois government of 1976 also shared this experience (Åsling 2001). The Swedish welfare state, which earlier had been widely regarded as a highly efficient organisation for social change, appeared to have reached a point of satiation and political inertia.

The present article tracks how these concerns—voiced by both the left and the right—translated into calls for an official investigation on the shifting preconditions for power. More specifically, it examines how these calls resulted in the launch of the Study of Power and Democracy in Sweden (*Utredningen om maktfördelning och demokrati i Sverige*) called *Maktutredningen* for short (henceforth 'the power investigation'). The background, activities and reception of the power investigation are analysed, from its beginning in 1985 to the delivery of its final report five years later, in 1990.

The power investigation had to negotiate two distinct expectations. On the one hand, it had a clear political mandate for 'exposing' private power in the interest of equality and justice. On the other, it was also implicitly tasked with studying ways of improving the exercise of public power in the interest of democracy and efficiency. Largely on account of this two-fold objective, the power investigation was criticised by some in the early 1990s for not having disclosed private power openly enough, while others complained that it had not shown how welfare state policies might be adapted to the challenges of globalisation and individualisation.

However, the lasting impact of the investigation should not be evaluated with regard to these two aspects alone, but must also be assessed for its role in reconceptualising the socio-political language of welfare state politics more generally. By probing new vocabularies of public service, participation and openness, the power investigation called attention to new ways of speaking about the welfare state. These vocabularies could be used to transcend the traditional dichotomies of past welfare state debates, often phrased in counter-concepts such as equality or efficiency, planning or liberty. The power investigation outlined a new self-understanding for the Swedish political elite, pointing away from the supposedly conformist, corporatist 'Swedish model' towards a more dynamic, flexible and participatory 'open society' (SOU 1990:44). Through its shaping of academic and public views of the Swedish welfare state, the power investigation exemplifies the power inherent in the right to investigate power.

Welfare State Criticism: From the Strong Society to the Concrete Society

During its most expansive phase in the 1960s and 1970s, SAP chairman and Swedish Prime Minister (1948–1969) Tage Erlander's dual concepts of *det starka samhället* ('the strong society') and *valfrihetens samhälle* ('the freedom of choice society') served as the primary guiding principles of the Swedish welfare state (Erlander 1962; 1976; Lindgren 2010). According to the first phrase, the state needs to be powerful enough to compensate for structural inequalities in society in order to bring about social security. Such compensation should be provided universally by means of progressive taxation and the generous provision of welfare, thereby facilitating true freedom of choice for as many citizens as possible. Sweden's success was often understood as a result of this policy of explicit social investment that sought to promote economic growth, together with social security (Andersson 2006; Erlander 1962; Myrdal 1960; Tingsten 1966).

While the reform policies were largely implemented by social democratic governments, they were typically processed through state committees in which opposition parties, popular movements, trade unions and relevant authorities were represented in a manner considered characteristic of the Scandinavian political system (Anton 1980; Aylott 2014; Elder, Arter, and Thomas 1982). While the welfare state sought to cope with the 'dissatisfaction of unsatisfied expectations', as Erlander (1962, 60) had called it in 1956, the pressure not only to provide better social security and more social welfare, but to do so in a more cost-efficient manner, motivated wide-scale 'structural rationalisation' of the Swedish economy, which in turn generated far-ranging social change.

Structural rationalisation enjoyed broad public support across the political spectrum. Yet, this consensus did not necessarily reflect the opinion of all groups, in particular the views of younger voters. Many were concerned with both the lingering shortcomings of Swedish society as well as the new risks posed by the modern welfare state. By the early 1970s, social scientists began to report on rising anti-establishment attitudes and declining membership in civil society organisations. A critical counter-concept emerged in opposition to the notion of the strong society, *betongsamhället*, 'the concrete society', indicating a cold, inflexible and sterile social environment, far removed from the ideals of care and equality held up by the welfare state. The strong society no longer appeared automatically conducive to freedom of choice as in Erlander's original conception (Almqvist and Glans 2001; Frenander 1998; Mellbourn 1986; Östberg 2009; Wiklund 2006).

Noting the growing criticism against the welfare state, leading social democrats such as Hans Esping and Måns Lönnroth concluded that social democracy ran the risk of ending up in 'an unfortunate defensive position' as a result of bourgeois parties trying to exploit popular dissatisfaction with 'power' that cut across the political spectrum (Åkerman 1969; Anners 1976; Esping and Lönnroth 1976, 14; Ortmark 1967). The SAP responded in the 1976 elections by promising a further expansion of the welfare state to promote social equality through economic democracy, but it lost to a bourgeois alliance for the first time in 44 years.

In the post-electoral analysis that followed the defeat, Rune Molin, Secretary of the traditionally social democrat Swedish Trade Union Confederation (*Landsorganisationen i Sverige*; LO), argued that long-term responsibility for the administration of the country will of necessity result in conflicts with various groups, who hold 'social democracy responsible for problems in advanced industrial society which really result from capitalism and lack of control over development' (1976, 370). Following the 1976 election, surveys conducted by political scientist Olof Petersson also showed that 'bureaucracy' and the unwieldy, impersonal and often anonymous state apparatus had been a decisive factor in the outcome of the elections, together with the political scandals that preceded the election, indicating power corruption and influential networks among the political elite (Gilljam and Nilsson 1984; Mellbourn 1986, 11 ff.; Petersson 1977, 199 ff.).[1]

Prior to the elections, Esping and Lönnroth had suggested that 'the party must treat the relationship between the citizens, the elected politicians, and the administration seriously'. In a motion made at the annual meeting of the Stockholm Labour Commune in 1976, they proposed that a specific investigation be launched to this end—one of the first suggestions of what would eventually become the power investigation (1976, 13 ff.).

A Forest of Red Pins: Who Has Power?

In the post-election analysis, social democrats often raised the problem of private power in the welfare state, especially through the media. This had also been emphasised in the new, more radical party programme of 1975 (SAP 1975). Molin concluded that the bourgeois victory would lead to 'a terrible power concentration of political, economic and media power in the same place'. But, he continued, this might not be entirely negative, as it might make more 'visible how economic power is in reality guilty of things social democracy has been blamed for' (1976, 375).

The incoming bourgeois government would also experience the limits of political power. Some critics argued that, while in opposition, the bourgeois parties had lost contact with important private power networks and organised social interests (Åsling 2001; Elvander 1966; Hermansson 1965). Others claimed that when those parties entered the corridors of power, they had been met by 'a forest of red pins', that is, a thoroughly politicised corps of civil servants, adjusted to social democratic ideals, whether they be members of SAP or not (Levin 1983). The criticism seemed to suggest that the social democrats somehow remained responsible, even when no longer in power (Enzensberger 1982; Gustafsson 1989).

The post-defeat social democrats mostly remained unrepentant, throwing this accusation back at the critics. The relative independence of the Swedish authorities, as laid out in the Constitution, meant that the government—social democratic or otherwise—could exercise little direct power over public administration. The social democratic response claimed that the SAP had sought precisely to avoid politicising the public administration. As a consequence of such moderation, the Swedish administrative bureaucracy had become a refuge for bourgeois civil servants with conservative world views and deeply entrenched power networks (Esping and Lönnroth 1976; Persson and Haste 1984).

Nevertheless, some prominent social democrats felt that there was some truth to the criticism. Party Secretary Bo Toresson, for example, noted that

> We social democrats have been organisation freaks.... Many of the reforms we implemented ... did not bring expected results. People did not recognise what we have said about planning legislation and social insurances when the ideas were translated into practical reality. (Toresson, as quoted in Persson and Haste 1984, 66)

Social democrats also perceived a genuine and growing tension between the demands for public services on the one hand and the calls for democracy and freedom of choice on the other. This tension emerged from an imbalance between Erlander's guiding principles of the welfare state, as for example Lennart J. Lundqvist noted:

> The ambitious welfare state seems trapped in a structural dilemma. The more you wish to place the emphasis on *performance*, i.e., the thorough and efficiently implemented provision of services, the more difficult it becomes to maintain the norm of *participation*, i.e., the demand for broad popular involvement in policy making and popular control of the implementation of decisions. The more that citizens share in welfare, the less they seem to share the democratic responsibility for the development of welfare. The larger the public sector, the more the citizens run the risk of becoming its clients rather than its controllers. (Lundqvist 1978, 365)

Ensuring the quality of the welfare state's performance would result in increasing dependence upon experts and complex non-personal systems, Lundqvist warned, running the risk of alienating and disenfranchising citizens.

Increasingly, the *styrproblem* ('steering problems') or *styrningsgapet* ('the steering gap') in the Swedish welfare state was experienced by both the social democrats and the bourgeois parties (Rothstein 1984). The question arose as to how any future government—bourgeois or social democratic—could avoid being blamed for things they were not responsible for, while at the same time wielding enough power over the public administration to implement the mandate of the electorate. A second question also arose: Who has usurped public power and how can it be taken back?

The bourgeois government answered this query in 1979 by placing liberal politician and political scientist Daniel Tarschys in charge of the Government Committee on Public Policy Planning (*Förvaltningsutredningen*), which was given the task of probing ways to improve the control and efficiency of public administration (SOU 1983:39). In 1983, the Centre for Business and Policy Studies (*Studieförbundet Näringsliv och Samhälle*; SNS) followed up by publishing two ambitious and well-received books that sought to analyse the failure of the bourgeois governments, telling a tale of systemic inertia and innovation difficulties of the Swedish model (Arvedson, Hägg, and Rydén 1983; Rydén 1983).[2] This critique should be placed in the context of the more ambitious attempt since the late 1970s, by organised business interests to use think tanks, research centres and publishing houses to present a different story about the rise and fall of the Swedish model than the previously dominant social democratic narrative (Boréus 1994).

Unwilling to let bourgeois parties score political points by exploiting the perception that state power had been usurped, social democrats eventually responded by taking their own initiative to launch a power investigation (Mellbourn 1986, 13; Persson and Haste 1984; Svensson 1993).

The Calls for a Power Investigation

The idea of a power investigation had already been raised before the 1976 elections (Esping and Lönnroth 1976, 14). However, not until the early 1980s were these demands expressed in the *Riksdag*. In a parliamentary debate on 30 November 1983 concerning certain constitutional questions, communist MP Jörn Svensson and social democrat MP Olle Svensson found themselves in agreement on the need for the political establishment to find a better way of steering the administration so that their political decisions achieved the desired results in society (*Riksdagens protokoll* 1983/84:36, 6§, Anf. 25, 26). Svensson went on to explain that knowledge was lacking about this key issue of democracy, but that Tarschys' (1978) research had proven that:

> "An autonomous [*självstyrande*, literally 'autocratic,' as distinct from the positively-coded *självständig*, e.g. 'independent'] administration cannot be the ideal. With too weak a government, we run the risk of ending up in a situation that the Norwegian power investigation has described as public governance without political control. (*Riksdagens protokoll* 1983/84:36, 6§, Anf. 26)."

On 11 January 1984, C. H. Hermansson, the long-standing chairman of the communist Left Party (*Vänsterpartiet kommunisterna*; VPK), put a motion before the *Riksdag* which claimed power had become more and more concentrated in Swedish society through the centralisation of public administration, business and organised social interest groups, while the *Riksdag* had lost power to the government. As a consequence, the distance between the governed and those who govern had increased. The individual citizen had become more and more isolated from political decision making. Noting that private power was described as growing in concentration while public power was assumed to be dispersing, Hermansson argued that these contradictory accounts of power relations in Swedish society necessitated a thorough analysis through a dedicated power investigation akin to the Norwegian power investigation that had delivered its final report in 1982 (Motion 1983/84:334).

In treating Hermansson's motion in October 1984, the Committee on the Constitution (*Konstitutionsutskottet*; KU) described the issues as 'important'. Nevertheless, it declared that such a power investigation would not be 'purposive', as the problems outlined in Hermansson's motion had either already been or were in the process of being studied by a number of other governmental investigations. Hence, the KU declined the motion in a decision on 8 October 1984 (KU 1984/85:5).

In January 1985, Hermansson and the Left Party returned with a renewed request for a power investigation (Motion 1984/85:290). Hermansson emphasised that a number of representatives of parties and organised social interests on the left and the right had expressed their support for a power investigation based on the Norwegian model, and there had been two parliamentary motions by the liberal People's Party (*Folkpartiet*; FP) and the SAP (Motion 1984/85:1508, 1984/85:473). However, Hermansson envisioned a parliamentary committee, rather than a scientific research group like the Norwegian power investigation (Motion 1984/85:290).

These motions were treated by the KU in a report to the Committee on Education on 28 March 1985. In a reversal of its previous standpoint, the KU now proposed that these issues needed to be researched. The KU explained that the government recently had declared that it would appoint a power investigation whose aim would be to map power in business, civil authorities, organisations and mass media and determine how public and private interests are 'interwoven' through these power relations. According to the KU, the Left Party MP's demands had thus already been met by the government's initiative to establish this scientific project. However, the communist member of the KU filed a minority report arguing that it would be essential in order to guarantee democratic control of the study to establish a parliamentary committee, including representatives of organised interests, rather than a scientific research group (KU 1984/85:7y).

The Power Investigation, 1985–1990

On 24 March 1985, only four days before the treatment of Hermansson's above-mentioned motion in the KU, Vice Prime Minister Ingvar Carlsson announced at a district conference of the Swedish Social Democratic Youth League (*Sveriges socialdemokratiska ungdomsförbund*; SSU) in Södertälje that the government would appoint a power investigation. This investigation would be conducted by 'qualified and independent researchers' over a relatively long period 'since one cannot uncover all the ramifications of power overnight', as he told the audience of young social democrats.[3]

In the spring of 1985, these seemingly academic questions were directly linked to the political contest between social democracy and an increasingly self-assertive bourgeois opposition that SAP leader Olof Palme warned would represent a *systemskifte* ('systemic shift') away from the Swedish model in favour of neo-liberalism of the Thatcherite kind (Anell and Carlsson 1985; Elmbrant 1989; 1993; Korpi and Åberg 1985; Östberg 2009).

As Carlsson emphasised in Södertälje, the prospect of such a shift made the task of the power investigation critical to the future of Swedish politics.[4]

The directives or terms of reference for the investigation were established on 27 June 1985, and Carlsson informed the media on 28 June 1985 that the government had decided to appoint a committee of inquiry, whose task was to study the distribution of power and democracy in Sweden. In a press release on that day, Carlsson explained that the power investigation would be facing an enormous task, since power was one of the most pervasive, yet most contested concepts of the social sciences. Nevertheless, the main question would be simple and direct. 'Who has power—and why? And how can more people get a real chance to decide not only about their own lives, but about social development as a whole, too?' The investigation would not only influence social science research and debate, 'but the entire political life. It is really about the fact that we want to deepen knowledge of the preconditions of democracy.'[5] Three main questions were singled out:

1. The distribution of power and the influence of the citizenry.
2. Power and influence within four delimited areas of society: business, the public sector, organisations, and public opinion.
3. Are citizens' opportunities for insight and control increasing?[6]

The terms of references for the investigation had been drawn up by Måns Lönnroth (Dir 1985, 36).[7] Lönnroth had been one of the first to call for a power investigation in 1976 and had since studied energy policies at the Swedish Secretariat for Future Studies. The directives were heavily influenced by the idea that power had become more *otydlig* ('opaque', 'obscure', 'unclear'), making it more difficult to prove causality, assign accountability and govern society in general. This was becoming a crucial problem for democratic welfare state governance in the post-industrial age, particularly in view of individualisation and internationalisation.

The experts conducting the power investigation were to analyse the relationship between administration, business and interest organisations—'iron triangles', as they were called in Norway—and the entanglement between the public and private sectors. The formation of public opinion was also to be studied. Carlsson urged that the power investigation function as an expert commission whose findings would form the basis for parliamentary decisions. In his press release, Carlsson noted that the problem of power looked different, depending upon one's political and ideological views. For this reason, the experts had been selected on the basis of their scientific competence and not on account of their political values. Carlsson said that other researchers whose work addressed power structures in Swedish society, but who would not be included in the power investigation, should not feel disadvantaged, as they too would be better able to contribute their research findings once the investigation was under way.

The task of coordinating arrangements for the power investigation fell to the Prime Minister's Office. Soon after the press release, political scientist Olof Petersson, well-known for his statistical surveys and analysis of the election results in 1976, was assigned to lead the power investigation. Petersson was later joined by economist Inga Persson (later Persson-Tanimura), Norwegian political scientist Johan P. Olsen, and historian Yvonne Hirdman.[8]

At a time when the Swedish system of committees came under pressure to cut spending and deliver reports at a faster pace than before, the power investigation not only stands out for the scale of its commitment with a budget of 33 million SEK over five years, but also with regard to the unorthodox disbursement of those means. The government decided on 27 February 1986 that the investigation's budgetary allocation was to be managed by Uppsala University. The project was scheduled to conclude in the summer of 1990, one year before the national elections in 1991.[9]

The output of the investigation was impressive and corresponded to the resources directed at the task. Over time, 142 social science researchers were connected to the project—the list of collaborators reads like a *Who's Who* of Swedish social science at the time—resulting in 125 publications of various kinds (SOU 1990:44, 427–44). The main publications range from traditional sociological surveys on the recruitment, education, living conditions and opinions of citizens and elites, to classical political science studies of party politics, political behaviour and public administration. For example, the Katrineholm Study followed up on earlier Swedish sociological research in tracking the microcosm of a middle-sized Swedish town that could be seen as representative of the country as a whole (Åberg 1990). Other studies sought to chart, for example, private ownership in Swedish industry and the contact network of government officials (Eidem and Skog 1991; Petersson 1989b), while an advertised study of 'the Swedish power elite' failed to materialise (SOU 1990:44, 430).

However, the power investigation possibly served its most important role as an incubator for innovative forms of research on topics little known previously. Empirically and theoretically innovative approaches included, for example, the study of the discrimination of women and immigrants (Ålund and Schierup 1991; Hirdman 1988; Persson 1990), language and metaphors for society and power (Petersson 1987a, b, 1989a), the introduction as well as criticism of organisational theory and new management forms in public administration (Brunsson 1989; Brunsson and Olsen 1990; Czarniawska-Joerges 1988), and the increasingly important role of media for Swedish politics and society (Petersson and Carlberg 1990). Research into the historical origins and outcomes of Swedish consensual welfare state politics had a long-lasting impact, most notably political scientist Rothstein's (1988) study of Swedish corporatism and Hirdman's (1989) volume on 'social engineering' and 'Swedish people's home politics'.

The power investigation also helped to create national and international networks between social scientists, while familiarising a whole generation of social scientists with broad trends in their disciplines, research project management and transdisciplinary collaboration. Thus, it contributed to a panoptic, yet kaleidoscopic, image of Swedish society, which in its parts dealt with widely different aspects of social life, but taken together composed a sweeping portrait of sometimes conflicting, sometimes complementary, yet distinctly new, narratives about the nation, the welfare state and challenges ahead.

Not Seeing the Wood for the Trees: Where Is Power?

"But where is power? Who is responsible? The government blames the mistakes of the previous government. The previous government, in its turn, points to the economy. Are the businessmen therefore to blame? No, they answer, business freedom is being constrained, they answer. Now the trade unions and the state govern. But the politicians are less able to survey things and govern, claiming to be more and more dependent upon civil servants and the bureaucracy. But civil servants and trade unionists reject the accusation and point to all the decisions being made above their heads . . . . Thus the chain of guilt rattles away. Power is everywhere, but also nowhere. No one wants to be associated with power." (Petersson and Hirdman 1985, 2).

Cited above is chief power investigator Olof Petersson's description of the elusive character of the object of study in the autumn of 1985. It not only illustrates the complexity of the task before the power investigation, but also reflects the unwillingness to shoulder responsibility in a complex society. One senses a genuine bewilderment and uncertainty on the part of actors and scholars concerning the causal relations in society. Finally, it echoes the working hypothesis of 'obscure power', as expressed in the directives that guided the power investigation and was confirmed in its final report entitled *Demokrati och makt i Sverige* (Democracy and Power in Sweden; SOU 1990:44).

While generally in agreement with the emerging trend in Swedish social science and humanities towards social constructivism, the power investigation's confirmation of the theory of obscure power came as a disappointment to some. The left had suspected that private power and matching conservative power elites in the 'bourgeois' public administration and private business dominated Swedish society, while those on the right believed that public power and a kind of leftist power elite had 'politicised' public administration and popular movements. However, the power investigation now found that public and private power elites existed side by side in Sweden and that by balancing each other, the two had been generally beneficial for the largely consensual development of Swedish political culture and the Swedish welfare society.

The power investigation received considerable coverage in national media as can be seen in its press archive. The media generally concentrated upon three aspects. First, commentators discussed whether it had been legitimate for the Government to commission a study of power at all, and whether the investigation's findings could be seen as objective. Second, most journalists concluded that the power investigation had proven that the era of Swedish exceptionalism had ended, and that internationalisation would increasingly have to be taken into account in national policymaking. Third, most commentators agreed with the concluding report that the Swedish model had now finally become obsolete (SOU 1990:44, 407). Still, they disagreed on the features that had distinguished this social configuration and whether the change that had taken place presented a window of opportunity or a closed door for future political and social reform.[10]

Within the academic community, Swedish social scientists were generally supportive of the investigation's efforts, but found them often wanting in comparison with those of its Norwegian predecessor. While the power investigation skilfully introduced the cutting-edge notion of imprecise, relational and situational power into Swedish social science, some complained that the numerous empirical studies did not directly prove how this supposedly obscure power actually worked in business, politics, organisations and media (Niklasson 1992). The politically loaded question that had articulated the concerns set out in the directives, '*Who* has power?', had been replaced with the much more complex, but also seemingly more harmless question of '*Where* is power?'

Critics on the right thought that the power investigation had not probed the democratising role of private entrepreneurship and the promise of what today would be called corporate social responsibility. Jan-Erik Lane (1992), a political scientist at Oslo University, faulted the power investigation for not addressing the supposedly hegemonic position of the labour movement in Swedish politics and society.

Social scientists and politicians to the left and to the centre expressed dissatisfaction with the power investigation for often assuming that the market had a 'pluralising' effect upon the provision of public service, without taking into account the negative effects of consumerism and the issues of age, class and sustainability, that is, the interests and rights of coming generations. For example, one critic, Annika Åhnberg of the Left Party, noted that the power investigation had not analysed the way in which the members of the power investigation themselves exercised power in conducting the power investigation as representatives of government-commissioned science (Åhnberg 1992). Some critics on the right agreed, wondering whether it could be considered legitimate for the government to entrust a specific group of social scientists with studying such a crucial, yet elusive, phenomenon as power (Niklasson 1992).

From the perspective of the power investigation, these concerns could be relatively easily refuted. First, democratic politics should ideally generate continuous debates on the 'essentially contested' understanding of society. The power investigation did not aim to establish a consensus on the status of democracy and power in Sweden, but to promote precisely such a debate. Second, in the 1980s, Swedish social science was largely funded by the government, and none of the critics of the power investigation, who were often Swedish academics who had not participated in the study itself, suggested that Swedish social science in general was biased in favour of the Government because of its overall dependence upon government funding.

Swedish academics generally considered the Swedish power investigation less successful than its Norwegian precedent in raising awareness of power issues. Ironically, this was repeatedly stated by debaters while the investigation's findings were discussed in the public sphere. In fact, the debate that ensued mostly took place between academics and public intellectuals, rather than among politicians and citizens.[11]

With regard to the latter, one of the most debated contributions of the power investigation was Hirdman's (1989) study *Att lägga livet till rätta* (Putting Life Right). Her other contributions to the power investigation had already had an energising effect upon the debate regarding equality, gender and feminism in contemporary Swedish society. This book presented a critical reassessment of the communitarian, yet rationalistic morality of the Swedish welfare state, addressing the dark side of social control inherent in what was formerly the positively coded metaphor of *folkhemmet* ('the people's home'). The debate set the scene for contention over issues of power in terms of inclusion and exclusion, identity politics, integration and multiculturalism that followed in the 1990s and 2000s. Furthermore, Hirdman's work made a strong impression on public debate about the Swedish welfare state, both at home and abroad.

Much of the ensuing discussion concentrated upon the 'sins of the past' and did not link the contemporary demand for public control of power due to the economic and political crisis of the early 1990s with the crisis of the 1930s. A critic on the left, sociologist Göran Therborn, argued that the power investigation had failed to take into account the continuity between the supposedly illegitimate social engineering of the 1930s and the seemingly legitimate contemporary demands for public power to take control of social change. It was assumed that there was some kind of rift separating these two positions, something Therborn (1992) found difficult to justify.

Welfare State Retrenchment: From the Swedish Model to the Open Society

When the power investigation delivered its final report in the Summer 1990, it was poised to make a significant contribution to the upcoming election campaign. By then, however, many of the concerns, problems and questions, which had originally motivated the launching of the power investigation in 1985, had changed. Systemic and ideological welfare state criticism had been superseded by largely economic considerations in regard to the economic crisis in Spring 1990, Sweden's relations to the EEC/EU, and the aftermath of the political turbulence of the late 1980s, including the assassination of Prime Minister Palme in February 1986. To some extent, then, the power investigation did fit the familiar saying that one of the primary functions of publicly commissioned studies in Sweden has been to bury hot potatoes, even if this can hardly have been anticipated or desired.

The investigation's original concerns had largely been replaced by a widespread understanding that the crisis of the Swedish model was due to economic causes and required market-oriented solutions. Yet, the technical complexity of administering a more ambitious welfare state, financing it through mutual cooperation between capital and labour, and the legitimacy of the welfare state with its corporatism and the committee system (involving popular movements, interest groups and authorities alongside political parties) remained, creating two interlocked problems: on the one hand, the 'sectoralisation' through iron triangles that had usurped public power and, on the other, the preservation of private power networks that had co-opted public power. The intertwining of these two problems obscured power beyond recognition.

Both of these problems had played a decisive role in three calls for opening up politics and the public sector from above as well as from below that had preceded the launching of the power investigation: there had been public demands for more insight, influence, participation and local democracy in controlling the public sector, for example openness from below. When this demand was channelled through established party politics—both by the bourgeois parties and by the social democrats—it was largely transformed into the question of how politicians could gain or regain public power so that they could influence the authorities in the interest of the citizens (public opinion), for example openness from above. Here, the demand for renewal also linked up with the demand from the left for public scrutiny of private power concentration and its influence upon public power as well as with the demand from the right for a public check on the social democratic influence within the public sector.

When Ingvar Carlsson officially introduced the power investigation in June 1985, he stated that the expert opinions developed would form the basis for parliamentary decisions. However, the directives did not require that the power investigation provide any recommendations for policy implementation. Despite that, the final report did make a suggestion with regard to policy language, arguing that the corporatist Swedish model and its 'hierarchical' structure of social relations had become largely obsolete and a stumbling block to improved democracy. Adopting a more 'vertical' view of society instead would make it possible to replace the supposedly ailing Swedish model with a new image: that of Sweden as an 'open society' (Petersson 1987b, 1989a, 1989b; SOU 1990:44, 405–9). While the power investigators cautioned against overstating the difference between these two images, noting that the Swedish model had contained many dynamic and internally conflicting elements, the widespread acceptance of the open society as a catchword for the

Swedish political and social system (alongside the welfare state) has proven remarkably resilient and continues to structure public debate even today (Götz and Marklund, forthcoming).

Conclusion

The political impetus to the power investigation originated with the Left Party, and in particular Hermansson's long-standing concerns with the problem of increased concentration of private power in affluent welfare states—power that threatened to incapacitate state autonomy. To social democrats, the power investigation was presented as a way to continue the quest for combining democracy with efficiency, liberty and power in the Swedish welfare state, that is, to provide a solution to the steering problem, while simultaneously mapping private power concentrations that might need to be controlled. Through this dual focus, politicians and public administrators would as an added benefit, be able to learn from business how to exercise power in an increasingly volatile world.[12] Among bourgeois politicians, by contrast, the power investigation was seen as an instrument for detecting 'hidden' power structures in the public sector.

On the most basic level, then, the power investigation resulted from a growing concern that power, wherever it could be found, needed to be scrutinised. The 'iceberg of power' thesis that assumed that power had an inherent capacity of hiding itself, and the more hidden, the more dangerous, had entered Swedish political culture. At the same time, it confirmed the belief that the power elites were honest enough to commission their own scrutiny (Götz 2010). By probing different ways of navigating this tension, the power investigation played an important role in fusing bourgeois and social democratic languages of 'governance as scrutiny'. In rhetorically rejuvenating the Swedish style of governance, containing the bureaucracy critique, and providing new vocabularies of participation, public service and openness to replace the language of planning and rationalisation of the past, these manoeuvres bridged the ideological and rhetorical gap between bourgeois and social democratic policy that had widened during the previous 20 years. A promise was held out of pluralism and performance, liberty as well as security and justice, and representation together with responsibility.

From the 1990s and onwards, these vocabularies would become characteristic of 'post-political governance' (Garsten and Jacobsson 2013). They also played their part in establishing a new national narrative about the recent past of the Swedish welfare state and its possible future. In providing this 'thick description', the ideals of the universalistic welfare state continued to be embraced, while its means seemed more obsolete. Now, market-oriented alternatives could be allowed in the quest to achieve the long-standing goal of making welfare state politics more democratic and more efficient (Scharpf 1999). Paradoxically, the national optics of this research effort contradicted some of the tendencies towards individualisation and internationalisation it had itself identified and analysed, supporting the persistence of a weak, yet unifying vision of a 'national we' in view of rising global competition (Kettunen 2008).

The power investigation had no mandate to provide an authoritative view on power. Rather, it was tasked with amassing knowledge and contributed to the debate over Swedish democracy. Nowadays, no serious attempt at analysing or discussing the political and social development of post-industrial Sweden from the 1970s to the 1990s can ignore the impressive output of the power investigation or the interpretative effort of its main report. Perhaps the most significant, although unintentional, achievement of the power investigation was that it contributing to shaping the image of the past Swedish model (to which contemporary observers may look back with longing or discomfort, even in the 2010s) while embracing the notion of contemporary Sweden as moving towards becoming an open society.

The numerous individual studies commissioned by the power investigation are so nuanced and rich that they cannot be reduced to support either the position of welfare state critics or welfare state supporters. However, the overall output of the investigation has clearly contributed to cement the widespread public belief that a fundamental shift took place during the 1980s—one from the corporatist and allegedly more 'mechanical' welfare state of old, to the supposedly more 'dynamic' competition state of the present. Through its kaleidoscopic outlook, the power investigation tells us the intriguing story of a welfare state capable of change, despite all the claims of stagnation and inertia which preceded its commissioning, and directs our gaze from the Swedish model of the past to the open society of the future.

Notes

[1] This dissatisfaction seems to have been of a temporary character, however. Already in the early 1980s, public trust in and support of the public sector were again on the rise, as evidenced in sociological reports.

[2] Interview with Olof Petersson, 24 April 2013.

[3] Arbetarrörelsens arkiv och bibliotek, SSU:s arkiv, handlingar från SSU:s distriktskonferens i Södertälje den 24 mars 1985, Statsrådsberedningens pressmeddelande den 24 mars 1985 om tillsättandet av en maktutredning och om statsrådet Ingvar Carlssons tillkännagivande samma dag vid SSU:s distriktskonferens i Södertälje.

[4] Arbetarrörelsens arkiv och bibliotek, SSU:s arkiv, handlingar från SSU:s distriktskonferens i Södertälje den 24 mars 1985, Stolpar till Ingvar Carlssons tal.

[5] This had indeed been one of the original arguments against a scientific study and in favour of a parliamentary committee.

[6] Riksarkivet, Kommittéarkiv, Maktutredningen, YK 4108, Volym 1, Statsrådsberedningens pressmeddelande den 28 juni 1985 om maktutredningens uppdrag.

[7] Interview with Olof Petersson, 24 April 2013.

[8] Both Hirdman and Petersson expressed some surprise at having been offered the position on the power investigation, in both cases personally by Ingvar Carlsson. Interview with Yvonne Hirdman, 10 May 2012; Interview with Olof Petersson, 24 April 2013.

[9] Riksarkivet, Kommittéarkiv, Maktutredningen, YK4108, Maktutredningens redovisning den 21 augusti 1986 till justitiedepartementet.

[10] Riksarkivet, Kommittéarkiv, Maktutredningen, Pressklipp, YK 4108, Vols 25–34.

[11] Riksarkivet, Kommittéarkiv, Maktutredningen, Pressklipp, YK 4108, Vols 25–34.

[12] This resembles the way in which social reformers in the 1930s looked at the scientific management of industry in order to develop efficient means towards social engineering.

References

Åberg, R. 1990. *Industrisamhälle i omvandling: Människor, arbete och socialt liv i en svensk industristad från femtiotal till åttiotal*. Stockholm: Carlsson.

Åhnberg, A. 1992. "Vi måste bryta maktlöshetens strukturer." In *Lärdomar av maktutredningen*, edited by L. Niklasson, 127–134. Stockholm: Carlsson Bokförlag.

Åkerman, N. 1969. *Apparaten Sverige: Samtal med beslutsfattare i politik, ämbetsverk, företag*. Stockholm: Wahlström & Widstrand.

Almqvist, K., and K. Glans. 2001. *Den svenska framgångssagan?* Stockholm: Fischer.

Ålund, A., and C. -U. Schierup. 1991. *Paradoxes of Multiculturalism: Essays on Swedish Society.* Aldershot: Avebury.

Andersson, J. 2006. *Between Growth and Security: Swedish Social Democracy from a Strong Society to a Third Way.* Manchester: Manchester University Press.

Anell, L., and I. Carlsson. 1985. *Individens frihet och framtidens välfärdssamhälle: En diskussion av de två alternativen i svensk politik.* Stockholm: LO.

Anners, E. 1976. *Den socialdemokratiska maktapparaten.* Stockholm: Askild & Kärnekull.

Anton, T. J. 1980. *Administered Politics: Elite Political Culture in Sweden.* Boston, MA: Martinus Nijhoff.

Arbetarrörelsens arkiv och bibliotek. SSU:s arkiv.

Arvedson, L., I. Hägg, and B. Rydén, eds. 1983. *Land i olag.* Stockholm: SNS.

Åsling, N. G., ed. 2001. *Maktskifte: Regeringarna Fälldin och den politiska miljön i 1970-talets Sverige.* Stockholm: Ekerlid.

Aylott, N. fortcoming, 2014. "A Nordic Model of Democracy? Political Representation in Northern Europe." In *Models of Democracy in Nordic and Baltic Europe: Political Institutions and Discourses,* edited by N. Aylott. Aldershot: Ashgate.

Boréus, K. 1994. *Högervåg: Nyliberalismen och kampen om språket i svensk debatt 1969–1989.* Stockholm: Tiden.

Brunsson, N. 1989. *The Organization of Hypocrisy. Talk, Decisions and Actions in Organizations.* Chichester: John Wiley & Sons.

Brunsson, N., and J. P. Olsen, eds. 1990. *Makten att reformera.* Stockholm: Carlsson Bokförlag.

Czarniawska-Joerges, B. 1988. *To Coin a Phrase: On Organizational Talk, Organizational Control and Management Consulting.* Stockholm: The Economic Research Institute.

Dir 1985:36. Utredningen om maktfördelning och demokrati i Sverige. Beslut vid regeringssammanträde 1985–06–27.

Ehnmark, A., and P. O. Enquist. 1987. *Protagoras sats: På spaning efter det politiska förnuftet.* Stockholm: Norstedt.

Eidem, R., and R. Skog. 1991. *Makten över företagen.* Stockholm: Carlsson.

Elder, N., A. H. Thomas, and D. Arter. 1982. *The Consensual Democracies? The Government and Politics of the Scandinavian States.* Oxford: Martin Robertson.

Elmbrant, B. 1989. *Palme.* Stockholm: Författarförlaget Fischer & Rye.

Elmbrant, B. 1993. *Så föll den svenska modellen.* Stockholm: Fischer.

Elvander, N. 1966. *Intresseorganisationerna i dagens Sverige.* Lund: Gleerup.

Enzensberger, H. M. 1982. *Svensk höst. En reportageserie i Dagens Nyheter 1982.* Stockholm: Ordfront Förlag/ Dagens Nyheter.

Erlander, T. 1962. *Valfrihetens samhälle.* Stockholm: Tiden.

Erlander, T. 1976. *Tage Erlander. 1955–1960.* Stockholm: Tiden.

Esping, H., and M. Lönnroth. 1976. "En socialistisk statsförvaltning?" *Tiden* 69 (1): 12–20.

Frenander, A. 1998. *Debattens vågor: Om politisk-ideologiska frågor i efterkrigstidens svenska kulturdebatt.* Gothenburg: University of Gothenburg.

Garsten, C., and K. Jacobsson. 2013. "Post-political Regulation: Soft Power and Post-political Visions in Global Governance." *Critical Sociology* 39 (3): 421–437.

Gilljam, M., and L. Nilsson. 1984. *Svenska folket och den offentliga sektorn.* Gothenburg: University of Gothenburg.

Götz, N. 2010. "'Machtuntersuchung' als Selbstaufklärung: Merkmale einer Kulturpraktik." In *Vom alten Norden zum neuen Europa: Politische Kultur in der Ostseeregion,* edited by N. Götz, J. Hecker-Stampehl, and S. M. Schröder, 131–150. Berlin: Wissenschafts-Verlag.

Götz, N., and C. Marklund, eds. forthcoming. *The Promise of Openness.* Leiden: Brill.

Gustafsson, L. 1989. *Problemformuleringsprivilegiet: Samhällsfilosofiska studier.* Stockholm: Norstedt.

Hermansson, C. H. 1965. *Monopol och storfinans: De 15 familjerna.* Stockholm: Rabén & Sjögren.

Hirdman, Y. 1988. *Genussystemet: Teoretiska funderingar kring kvinnors sociala underordning.* Uppsala: Maktutredningen.

Hirdman, Y. 1989. *Att lägga livet till rätta: Studier i svensk folkhemspolitik.* Stockholm: Carlsson Bokförlag.

Kettunen, P. 2008. *Globalisaatio ja kansallinen me. Kansallisen katseen historiallinen kritiikki.* Tampere: Vastapaino.

Korpi, W., and R. Åberg. 1985. *Marknad eller politik? Om de politiska alternativen i 80-talets Sverige.* Stockholm: LO.

KU 1984/85:5. Konstitutionsutskottets betänkande om vissa grundlagsfrågor, m.m.

KU 1984/85:7y. Konstitutionsutskottets yttrande till utbildningsutskottet om utredning av maktförhållandena i Sverige.

Lane, J. -E. 1992. "Den politiska maktens logik." In *Lärdomar av maktutredningen*, edited by L. Niklasson, 25–45. Stockholm: Carlsson Bokförlag.

Levin, B. 1983. "En skog av röda nålar: Om politiseringen av departement och förvaltning." In *Makt och vanmakt*, edited by B. Rydén. Stockholm: SNS Förlag.

Lindgren, A. -M. 2010. *Tage Erlander och välfärden: Går verkligen Reinfeldt i Erlanders fotspår?* Stockholm: Arbetarrörelsens tankesmedja.

Lundqvist, L. J. 1978. "Demokratins Problem." *Tiden* 71 (6): 365–366.

Mellbourn, A. 1986. *Bortom det starka samhället. Socialdemokratisk förvaltningspolitik 1982–1985*. Stockholm: Carlssons Bokförlag.

Molin, R. 1976. "Tio dagar efter valet. Intervju med Rune Molin." *Tiden* 69 (7): 370–375.

Motion 1983/84:334. Carl-Henrik Hermansson (vpk) m.fl. Utredning om maktförhållandena i samhället.

Motion 1984/85:1508. Bengt Westerberg (fp) m.fl.

Motion 1984/85:290. Carl-Henrik Hermansson (vpk) m.fl. En utredning om maktförhållandena i samhället.

Motion 1984/85:473. Kurt Ove Johansson (s) och Lars Erik Lövdén (s) om behovet av en maktutredning.

Myrdal, G. 1960. *Beyond the Welfare State: Economic Planning in the Welfare State and its International Implications*. New Haven: Yale University Press.

Niklasson, L., ed. 1992. *Lärdomar av maktutredningen*. Stockholm: Carlsson Bokförlag.

Ortmark, Å. 1967. *Maktspelet i Sverige: Ett samhällsreportage*. Stockholm: Wahlström & Widstrand.

Östberg, K. 2009. *När vinden vände: Olof Palme 1969–1986*. Stockholm: Leopard.

Persson, I., ed. 1990. *Generating Equality in the Welfare State. The Swedish Experience*. Oslo: Universitetsforlaget.

Persson, J. -O., and H. Haste. 1984. *Förnyelse i folkhemmet*. Stockholm: Tiden.

Petersson, O. 1977. *Väljarna och valet 1976*. Stockholm: Statistiska Centralbyrån.

Petersson, O., ed. 1987a. *Maktbegreppet*. Stockholm: Carlsson Bokförlag.

Petersson, O. 1987b. *Metaforernas makt*. Stockholm: Carlsson Bokförlag.

Petersson, O. 1989a. *Makt i det öppna samhället*. Stockholm: Carlsson Bokförlag.

Petersson, O. 1989b. *Maktens nätverk. En undersökning av regeringskansliets kontakter*. Stockholm: Carlsson Bokförlag.

Petersson, O., and I. Carlberg. 1990. *Makten över tanken. En bok om det svenska massmediesamhället*. Stockholm: Carlsson Bokförlag.

Petersson, O., and Y. Hirdman. 1985. *Två föredrag om maktutredningen: TAMs, TBVs och TCOs tematräff om den politiska makten och folkstyret den 5 december 1985*. Uppsala: Maktutredningen.

Riksarkivet, Kommittéarkiv, Maktutredningen. YK 4108, Vols 1–34.

Riksdagens protokoll 1983/84:36.

Rothstein, B. 1984. "Gustav Möller, välfärdsstaten och friheten." *Tiden* 77 (10): 599–605.

Rothstein, B. 1988. *State and Capital in Sweden: The Importance of Corporatist Arrangements*. Uppsala: Maktutredningen.

Rydén, B., ed. 1983. *Makt och vanmakt: Lärdomar av sex borgerliga regeringsår*. Stockholm: SNS.

SAP (Sveriges socialdemokratiska arbetareparti). Program, Fastställd av 1975 års partikongress. http://snd.gu.se/sv/vivill/party/s/program/1975

Scharpf, F. W. 1999. *Governing in Europe: Effective and Democratic?* Oxford: Oxford University Press.

SOU 1983:39. *Politisk styrning – administrativ självständighet*, Betänkande av Förvaltningsutredningen. Stockholm: Liber/Allmänna förlaget.

SOU 1990:44. *Demokrati och makt i Sverige. Maktutredningens huvudrapport*. Stockholm: Allmänna förlaget.

Svensson, O. 1993. *Maktspel synat. På Erlanders, Palmes och Carlssons tid*. Stockholm: Norstedt.

Tarschys, D. 1978. *Den offentliga revolutionen*. Stockholm: LiberFörlag.

Therborn, G. 1992. "Guide Petersson och makten i det moderna." In *Lärdomar av maktutredningen*, edited by L. Niklasson, 70–85. Stockholm: Carlsson Bokförlag.

Tingsten, H. 1966. *Från idéer till idyll: Den lyckliga demokratien*. Stockholm: Norstedt.

Wiklund, M. 2006. *I det modernas landskap: Historisk orientering och kritiska berättelser om det moderna Sverige mellan 1960 och 1990* [In the landscape of modernity: Historical orientation and critical narratives about modern Sweden between 1960 and 1990]. Eslöv: Östlings bokförlag Symposion.

Three Nordic Power Investigations on the Repercussions of the European Union on Sovereignty and Democracy

ANN-CATHRINE JUNGAR
Södertörn University, Huddinge, Sweden

ABSTRACT *Public inquiries into the state of democracy and power were undertaken in three Scandinavian states—Norway, Denmark and Sweden—on the threshold of the twenty-first century. The parliamentary directives identified globalization and, above all, the effects of European integration as the main challenges to popular rule in these three small democracies. The Scandinavian power investigations arrived at different conclusions about the impact of European integration on national sovereignty and on the distribution of power in the respective societies, and each country saw their problem differently. The Swedish report acknowledged minor difficulty with regard to the distribution of power; the Norwegian investigation concluded on a bleak note; whereas the Danish conclusion was affirmative and was self-conscious of being a European role model. The article attributes national differences to different normative conceptions of sovereignty and to the historical and institutional character of the three states' relationship with the EU.*

Beginning in 1997, the Danish, Norwegian and Swedish parliaments each conducted its own inquiry on power and democracy.[1] What one might have expected to become a proof of affinity of Scandinavian political cultures became the very opposite. However, when the results were presented in 2003, the investigations in Denmark and Norway delivered diametrically opposed interpretations on the state of democracy. Whereas democracy appeared alive and legitimacy of the political system consolidated in Denmark, these elements seemed to have eroded in Norway (Makt- og demokratiutredningen 2003; Togeby et al. 2003).[2] The Swedish inquiry, whose conclusion had been published three years earlier, took a middle-ground position in its evaluation of the state of democracy in Sweden (Demokratiutredningen 2000; cf. Strandberg 2006, 537).

The differences between the interpretations of how recent societal changes had affected the seemingly similar Nordic welfare states were regarded as surprising (Karvonen 2004, 423). A thematic issue on the Nordic power investigations in the *Journal of European Public Policy* in 2006 asked whether the variations were not artefacts caused by different research designs and methods, and their conceptualizations and measurements of democracy and power. Another suggestion was that the presumed similarity between Nordic countries might have been exaggerated and therefore misled expectations (Strandberg 2006, 537). No definitive answers were provided at the time, but an appeal was made for further examination of the scholarly analysis on power and democracy. This article provides some tentative explanations of why there were such different reactions to the Scandinavian inquiries into internationalization and European integration in the three Scandinavian states with regard to perceived impact on national sovereignty and popular rule.

The power investigations were to a large extent dedicated to scrutiny of the repercussions of globalization. Particular attention was paid to the effects of the EU on power relationships and on democratic rule within member states or EU-associated states. Consequently, the aim of this article is to investigate how European integration and the internationalization of law were perceived, narrated and analysed in three official investigations of power and democracy in Denmark, Norway and Sweden on the threshold of the twenty-first century. These scholarly investigations were motivated by perceived challenges facing the Nordic democracies that needed to be addressed, understood, and possibly legitimized to the many citizens in the Scandinavian states sceptical of the EU (Miles 1996; Miljan 1977; Oskarsson 1996; Pesonen 1998). European integration has historically been a divisive issue within the three Scandinavian electorates. Narrow and competitive referenda on EU membership were held in Denmark and Norway in 1973 and in Sweden and Norway in 1994. Whereas Denmark and Sweden joined the EU, Norway never did. Denmark and Sweden have also held referenda on joining the Eurozone in 2000 and 2003, a move that was rejected by the voters in both countries. Since the EU has been a divisive issue within political parties and government coalitions of the Scandinavian states, it has been decoupled from ordinary politics, for instance, by popular referenda on the membership and the euro.

The commercialization, individualization, judicalization and weakened capacity of political parties and organizations to link citizens to political processes were a few of the challenges identified in the directives of the three commissions on power and democracy. Above all, the effects of globalization and the repercussions of European integration on small states were prioritized issues in the inquiries. This article suggests that their surprisingly divergent conclusions did not stem from different factual analysis of how international institutions—whether the EU or international law—impacted on the political systems, but can rather be ascribed to the three states' historical legacies in relation to the EU and different normative points of departure on the modes of operation of sovereignty and popular rule in increasingly internationalized political structures.

The Mission of the Inquiries

Public commissions and hearings with the participation of representatives from political institutions, political parties, the civil administration, and civil society are a vital part of the Nordic consensual decision-making model and a symbol of the openness of these societies (Bergh and Erlingsson 2009, 71 ff.). Major revisions of policies and problems requiring solutions are often met by setting up commissions tasked with collecting information, conducting deliberations and suggesting policy reforms. These commissions can be more or less independent with regard to the political institutions in terms of the character of the mandate, the working methods and the composition of the commissions.

Unlike other types of public inquiry, the commissions discussed here were not intended to draft policy proposals and legislative measures, but rather to reflect more generally on their respective societies. As the aim of the three inquiries was to provide a narrative on the condition of popular rule, they were exercises in persuasive power. The end of the Cold War and the dramatic international transformation it brought about, but also domestic developments at the end of the twentieth century, made the Norwegian and Swedish power investigations of the 1970s and 1980s seem outdated. The fall of the bipolar world order, increased horizontal and vertical European integration, changing forms of civic participation in politics, and citizens' growing distrust in political institutions and political parties all contributed to the wish for a new understanding of power and democracy. By the second half of the 1990s, it was considered time for a renewal of publicly commissioned scholarly analysis of these issues.

All three investigations were initiated by the national parliaments in the respective countries. Norway and Denmark launched power investigations according to the then established model of scholarly audits. The Swedish committee received a more limited mandate than those of the other countries or the previous Swedish power investigation. While most of the studies produced by the Swedish investigation were written by scholars, the committee itself was populated by legislators who also assumed responsibility for the final report. However, the overall working modes were similar, relying on scholarly research, organizing seminars and holding public hearings for a wider audience. While usually written by scholars, the publications of the power investigations were intended for the general public, not primarily the academic community. In reviews of the three inquiries, it was observed that no new theoretical or empirical insights were presented, but that existing knowledge was set into a broader frame of analysis (Karvonen 2004, 423).

The scope of the mandates of these commissions was reflected in the titles of the final reports. The result of the Danish power investigation was entitled *Magt og demokrati i Danmark* (Power and Democracy in Denmark) and that of the Norwegian investigation *Makt og demokrati* (Power and Democracy). The more narrow focus of the Swedish commission on one issue is implicit in the title of its final report: *En uthållig demokrati* (A Durable Democracy; Demokratiutredningen 2000; Makt- og demokratiutredningen 2003; Togeby et al. 2003).

Nordic Democracies and European Integration

Globalization, internationalization and, in particular, European integration were identified as developments to which the commissions were to pay special attention. The Scandinavian countries (along with Finland) are often grouped together as representatives of a distinct Nordic democratic model, characterized by a well-functioning welfare state, consensual politics and transparent democratic processes (Allardt 1981; Esaiasson and Heidar 2000; Esping-Andersen 1990; Katzenstein 1985; Kurunmäki and Strang 2010; Peterson 1994). On the one hand, the fact that they share characteristics pertaining to their political institutions, party structures, welfare state organization and economic context may lead one to presume convergence in their societal analysis. Similarly, similar narratives could be expected in their power investigations as the adaptation pressures emanating from the EU are presumably similar (Hanf and Soetendorp 1998, 4–6; Mény, Muller, and Quermonne 1996, 9 ff.; Olsen 2002, 932 ff.). However, as the three Scandinavian states have their own particular relationship to the EU, different impacts of European integration could be expected. Denmark and Sweden have been full member states of the European Economic Community (EEC) and its successor, the EU, since 1973 and 1995, respectively. Thus, they joined the European integration project at different stages of its vertical and horizontal institutional development, and might therefore have become socialized into the European structures differently. Norway is merely associated with the EU through the European Economic Area (EEA) agreement. The effects of European integration and perceived adaptation pressures emanating from the EU on its members might be related to the type of association and the timing of membership of the three Scandinavian states.

When Denmark joined the EEC in 1973, it rapidly gained a reputation as a troublemaker. The national parliament, the Folketing, kept tight control on the ministers negotiating in the Council. EU Commission Chair Jacques Delors is known for having stated that 'the EEC has 13 members, the 12 Member States and the Danish EEC Committee' (Jungar, forthcoming). Denmark has held several referenda on EU issues (Single European Act 1986; Maastricht Treaty 1992 and 1993; Treaty of Amsterdam 1998; the Euro 2000) and has consequently experienced intense domestic political debates on the development of European integration. This has spread tremors around Europe and inspired citizens in other member states to question the elite-driven European project. Over time, the Danish citizenry has grown accustomed to and socialized into the EU. The Danes express the greatest degree of identification with the EU among the Scandinavian states (Togeby et al. 2003, 317). However, that does not imply that they particularly embrace integration-friendly or federal attitudes.

Sweden joined the EU in 1995, after a narrowly decided referendum. In all, 51.3% of those participating in the ballot voted 'yes' to membership, something that cast a shadow over the Swedish EU debate in the following years. The public discussion was more focused on Sweden's membership in the EU as such than on which policies the country should pursue within EU institutions (Johansson 1999, 9 ff.; von Sydow 1999, 81 ff.). The major political parties—the Social Democrats (*Socialdemokraterna*) and the Conservatives (*Moderaterna*)—were internally divided over the EU (the latter less so), whereas the Left Party and the Greens requested in their respective party programmes that Sweden exit the EU. The Greens removed this paragraph in 2008, when they formed an alliance with the Social Democrats and the Left Party to challenge the centre-right government coalition. The Swedes voted 'no' to the European Monetary Union (EMU) in a referendum in 2003, and they remain among the more EU-critical citizens in Europe.

After two failed referenda on membership in the EEC/EU (1972 and 1994), Norway is associated with the EU through the EEA. This agreement refers to the free movement of goods, services, persons and capital, and also covers cooperation in other important areas such as research and development, education, social policy, the environment, consumer protection, tourism and culture. Some policy areas are excluded, such as agriculture and fisheries policies (although the agreement contains provisions on various aspects of trade in agricultural and fish products), customs union, trade policy, foreign and security policy, justice and home affairs (yet the remaining member countries of the European Free Trade Association (EFTA), to which Norway belongs, are part of the Schengen area), and the EMU. This particular arrangement, intended for a transitional period leading to full membership, means that Norway is formally obliged to follow EU regulations and legislation in numerous policy fields without being able to influence the legislative processes: the country is not represented in the EU decision-making bodies such as the Commission, the Council of Ministers and the European Parliament. However, the Norwegian administration has regular contacts with EU institutions, most notably the Commission, which prepares and monitors the implementation of EU legislation. While the EU has worked to the advantage of civil servants in terms of access to networks and information, it has de-coupled Norwegian parliamentarians from the EU policy-making process.

National Sovereignty

The scope of national sovereignty and self-determination is intimately related to internationalization and globalization. These processes have been accompanied by lively debates on the power of states and their survival in an increasingly transnational environment. The problem is whether states are capable of deciding their own destiny any longer, or whether their ability to tackle societal issues that transgress national borders is improving. Ultimately, this is a question of a vertical shift of power from states to international organizations and transnational actors (Eriksen and Fossum 2000). Whereas the conclusion of the Norwegian power investigation was that national sovereignty was impaired, the Danish investigation claimed that the question as to the state of national sovereignty was misleading. The Swedish democracy inquiry claimed that globalization exerted adaptation pressure on the nation state and societal institutions, restricting national self-determination. However, its evaluation of this development remained politically balanced: 'The perception of the effects of globalization is ultimately dependent on political values' (Demokratiutredningen 2000, 67). These divergent interpretations do not result nor can they be derived from significant factual differences; rather, they emanate from discrete normative points of departure regarding how sovereignty could and should be conceived of in an increasingly globalized political environment.

The divergent conclusions of the Norwegian and Danish investigations did, in fact, mirror two opposed theoretical perspectives on the impact of European integration and the internationalization of law on national sovereignty. On the one hand, integration is seen as gradually undermining the state, since more and more policy areas are intertwined with one another (Haas 1958, 1964, 1992; Stone Sweet and Brunell 1998). As EU legislation has a direct effect on and precedence over national legislation in a growing number of policy areas, the state is no longer considered sovereign. Moreover, the use of majority voting has increased, which means that a member state can be voted down in the Council but nevertheless has to follow common EU rules. In this sense, formal sovereignty of the state has weakened.

On the other hand, it is maintained that the actual development of European integration up until the present has strengthened the nation state (Moravcsik 1994, 1998). From this perspective, sovereignty is reformulated as problem-solving capacity; it is not conceived of as self-determination through non-involvement in the national decision-making process. The nation-states are seen as having delegated parts of their sovereignty to the EU with the aim of increasing their problem-solving capacity and their influence on policymaking in an increasingly interdependent world (Milward 1992). Hence, the EU appears as an instrument for dealing with political problems that states cannot control by themselves.

The Norwegian investigation stated that national self-determination had been severely restricted: the rhetorical question 'Is Norway any longer a sovereign state?' was answered with a clear 'no' (Østerud, Engelstad, and Selle 2003, 53). Formal sovereignty is challenged above all by the internationalization of the Norwegian legal system. The judicialization of politics has constantly expanded and, according to the Norwegian power investigation, political decision making has been handed over to international courts and other legal institutions. Accordingly, interest struggles are increasingly pursued as legal struggles by groups and individuals. Moreover, European integration has been advanced by judicial activism and is not fully in the hands of the member states. The Norwegian power investigation concluded that judicalization in this sense did not indicate a strengthening of the rule of law, but rather a reshuffling of political power from states and political representatives to international rules and institutions.

The Norwegian power investigation made the following claim: 'The wider implication of the internationalisation of law is that representative popular rule has cut its own wings. This can be attributed to the fact that both *internationalisation* and *human rights* have great normative power in our time' (Østerud, Engelstad, and Selle 2003, 53). With the EEA Treaty, restrictions on sovereignty have been imposed, as EU member states make laws that apply in Norway, according to the power investigation. The EEA Treaty means that Norway is bound by international law to harmonize all statutes within the framework of the treaty, even if the law of the EU is not automatically binding or supreme in relation to national law. Theoretically, Norway can refuse to adopt EU legislation, but it is politically difficult for a small state not to abide by rules made by the EU, even as a non-member. To be trapped in what is sometimes seen as the waiting room to the EU implies a two-fold democratic deficit. Not only is the EU characterized by democratic shortcomings in itself, but as a non-member state associated with the EU, Norway is not even capable of influencing this weakly democratic organization, whose policy it permits to become legally binding upon it. Moreover, international conventions on human rights and the constitutionalsation and judicalization of the political sphere have further circumvented national self-determination and democratic majority rule (Østerud, Engelstad, and Selle 2003, 53).

The Danish power investigation acknowledged that national sovereignty had been circumscribed, but suggested that the loss of self-determination was compensated for by an increase in problem-solving capacity. All in all, Danish democracy seemed to be doing well—'surprisingly well', as the final report stated (Togeby et al. 2003, 402). Moreover, it was claimed that the traditional idea of sovereign statehood was obsolete when a country was integrating with other international organizations in which power is pooled:

> The concept of national sovereignty cannot any longer be maintained . . . . It is under pressure. And that would have been the case in any circumstance. The EU can be seen as the main cause to reduced national self-determination, but European integration can also be conceived of as a solution to problems that individual states cannot deal with alone, that is, European integration is conceived of as a countermeasure against growing globalisation. (Togeby et al. 2003, 319)

While the Danish power investigation acknowledged the limitations on sovereignty as a consequence of EU membership, it maintained that the loss of sovereignty was less extensive than anticipated (Togeby et al. 2003, 319 ff.).

Obviously, there are problems with transparency and accountability within the EU, since neither its executive (the Commission) nor part of the legislative powers (the Council of Ministers, and the European Parliament) can collectively be held accountable by the people. In the Danish case, national sovereignty is not portrayed as lost, as is the case in the Norwegian investigation, but rather as 'lent out'. Hence, it is implicitly assumed that competencies member states have delegated to common European institutions can formally be withdrawn (Togeby et al. 2003, 308 ff.). Although less so now than when it was written, this seems to be a rhetorical trick based on a judgment by the German Federal

Court on 12 October 1993 on the compatibility of Germany's constitution with the Maastricht Treaty. The Federal Court declared that member states (and indirectly national parliaments) were responsible for and still maintained control over EU treaties, even though legislative capacities had been delegated to the EU by the member states. Thus, the EU was not seen as a federal state; instead, its members were regarded as the 'masters of the treaties' who could still determine the constituting rules of the organization.

The Swedish audit of democracy published its final report three years before the other commissions and was more moderate in its conclusions with regard to national sovereignty. The experience of being associated with the EU through the EEA agreement in the period 1992–1995, before becoming a full member state, was taken as a point of departure in the assessment of the impact of the EU on democracy. It was regarded as 'an order that from a democratic point of view has more disadvantages than full membership' (Demokratiutredningen 2000, 119). As the Swedish committee saw it, the EU was relatively open as an international organization, and it was therefore to be considered 'a democratic loss if the decision making that now takes place in the EU would be transferred to diplomatic and other negotiation structures' (Demokratiutredningen 2000, 119). The analysis of the legitimacy of the EU arose from a need to balance what is described as 'issue politics', on the one hand, and 'democratic politics', on the other. The argument was that citizen power would decrease if Sweden were to abstain from the possibilities that the EU offers to influence actively societal processes that affect citizens. The weakening of democratic procedures was seen as compensated for by the fact that influence over policymaking was enhanced. The Swedish commission therefore arrived at a similar conclusion as the Danish investigation some years later: there was a trade-off between national self-determination and democracy, and these concepts needed to be reconceptualized in order efficiently to confront and influence cross-border societal phenomena. With its focus on democracy and citizens' influence, the Swedish inquiry was more concerned with how the delegation of decision-making competencies to international institutions could be controlled by citizens, and therefore paid much attention to the strengthening of democratic procedures within the EU (Demokratiutredningen 2000, 69).

A Domestic Reshuffling of Power

Internationalization and globalization reshuffle power relations vertically between states and international institutions and actors. However, the internationalization of politics also transforms power relations horizontally within states. It is often maintained that internationalization, in general, and European integration, in particular, lead to domestic centralisation of power (Moravcsik 1994). Institutions and individuals with access to decision making on the European level either in the Commission's preparatory phases or later during negotiations in the Council of Ministers gain increased influence over political decision making domestically. Governments and civil servants benefit at home from their access to and control of information with regard to European decision making. From this perspective, democracy is weakened: uneven access to decision making on the EU level makes broad and informed participation impossible, and the role of parliament is reduced to reacting passively to government initiatives. It is often difficult to control how national representatives act and what positions they pursue in various EU entities. The EU level of governance emerges as an increasingly attractive political arena if those with access to the European decision-making apparatus are able to take advantage of this domestically at the expense of the political opposition and organized interests. The latter, along with political parties as well as civil servants, would then be inclined to cooperate to a greater extent across national borders and pursue common interests on the EU level, rather than influence policymaking in their home countries. This would gradually impoverish political discussion—and democracy—in the nation-state.

In all three Scandinavian investigations, the national parliament was considered the political institution that had lost the most power in consequence of integrating into the EU (for scholarly studies confirming this finding, see Ahlback-Öberg and Jungar 2009; Jungar 2009). Moreover, there was agreement that the executive and the civil administration had been strengthened. With regard to EU legislation that later had to be adopted into national legislation by the national parliaments, the Swedish final report observed that 'a considerable shift of power from the parliament to the government has occurred. The Swedish government—together with other member-state governments—is the legislator in practice' (Demokratiutredningen 2000, 115).

The Danish power investigation, too, recognized the loss of parliamentary control over EU policies: membership in the EU was explicitly seen as 'the greatest challenge for the Danish parliament in modern times'. When Denmark joined the EEC in 1973, the Folketing relinquished parts of its sovereignty as a legislator which in a democratic nation-state belongs to the parliament (Damgaard 1990, 1992; Jensen 2003). Over time, more sovereignty was transferred (Togeby et al. 2003, 129). However, the power investigation noted that the Danish parliament retained strong instruments with which to monitor and control EU policymaking. It issued binding mandates for cabinet ministers negotiating in the EU and scheduled regular meetings with the executive. Even though the situation could be improved by inviting sectoral parliamentary committees, the Danish Folketing was seen as a model for the parliaments of other EU members (Togeby et al. 2003, 313). Sweden, Finland, and a majority of the legislatures in the Central and East European member states have followed the Danish model of a mandating parliament (Jungar 2009, forthcoming).

The Norwegian power investigation concluded that the power of its parliament had diminished. It also held the most pessimistic view on this subject since its 'major conclusion ... was that representative democracy is eroding' (Selle and Østerud 2006, 552). The democratic chain of delegation had been broken and representative democracy weakened (Østerud, Engelstad, and Selle 2003, 80–9). The democratically elected national parliamentarians had been cut off from policymaking and opportunities for influence, whereas administrative channels were empowered by the EU policy-making processes. According to the Norwegian investigation the 'EU, the bureaucracy, and experts formulate central parts of Norwegian policies in practice' (Østerud, Engelstad, and Selle 2003, 93).

Conclusion

The internationalization of policymaking and European integration were the main concerns motivating the renewed public analysis of power and democracy in Denmark, Norway and Sweden in the end of the 1990s. The three investigations departed from similar problem descriptions, but ended up with divergent analyses and interpretations of the consequences of internationalization and European integration. The response to these challenges by the Swedish inquiry was pragmatic, the Norwegian investigation drew very pessimistic conclusions, and the Danish investigation took an affirmative position that viewed its country as a European role model.

The tentative explanation for these striking differences among politically and culturally similar small states is not primarily due to different factual contexts, but rather can be found in the historical legacies and present status of these states with regard to European integration. The current development of multilevel policy process contributes to an increased complexity and impenetrability in the three Scandinavian nations, all of which have historically been homogeneous unitary states. The vertical power sharing, judicial review of policymaking that accompanied integration into the EU structures, and international law has altered political processes and transformed the democratic chains of delegation. The exercise of popular sovereignty has also changed and the central role of the national parliaments has diminished, but in different ways, according to the three Scandinavian power investigations.

· Denmark and Sweden, as full members of the EU, have successfully adapted to the pressures of growing internationalization. Whereas the Norwegian power investigation depicted development in the direction of transnational governance in terms of a zero-sum game in which internationalization hollowed out national sovereignty, the Swedish and Danish investigations perceived that what had been lost in formal sovereignty had been gained in problem-solving capacity. The particular affiliation of Norway with the EU as a policy-taker that is unable to act as a policy maker is one significant reason for the difference. It has made it more difficult for the Norwegian power investigation to claim like the Danish and Swedish inquiries, that a loss of sovereignty has been compensated for by greater influence over policymaking.

Notes

[1] The Danish and the Norwegian inquiries worked within the then established tradition of 'power investigations'; both produced final reports on 'Power and Democracy'. The Norwegian investigation was even formally titled 'Power and Democracy Investigation'. The name of the Swedish inquiry was 'Democracy Investigation'; it was not framed as a power investigation and remained ultimately in the hands of politicians. However, as it existed parallel with the other investigations for some years and as it worked on related topics, it has frequently been compared to the other two investigations. For the purpose of this article, it is therefore treated as a power investigation.

[2] Two of the five members of the Norwegian investigation were present in this volume with dissenting statements, one of which advocated a more positive view of the challenges of Europeanization and globalization. The three representatives of the majority line published, in addition to the official report, a more comprehensive unofficial synopsis (Østerud, Engelstad, and Selle 2003). This article refers to both the official and the unofficial final reports when referring to the conclusions of the Norwegian power investigation.

References

Ahlbäck-öberg, S., and A. -C. Jungar. 2009. "The Influence of National Parliaments Over Domestic European Union Policies." *Scandinavian Political Studies* 32 (3): 359–381.

Allardt, E. 1981. *Nordic Democracy: Ideas, Issues, and Institutions in Politics, Economy, Education, Social and Cultural Affairs of Denmark, Finland, Iceland, Norway, and Sweden.* Copenhagen: Det danske selskab.

Bergh, A., and G. Erlingsson. 2009. "Liberalization without Retrenchment: Understanding the Consensus on Swedish Welfare State Reforms." *Scandinavian Political Studies* 32: 71–93.

Damgaard, E. 1990. *Parlamentarisk Forandring i Norden.* Oslo: Universitetsforlaget.

Damgaard, E. 1992. *Parliamentary Change in the Nordic Countries.* Oslo: Universitetsforlaget.

Demokratiutredningen. 2000. *En uthållig demokrati! Politik för folkstyrelse på 2000-talet* [The Democratic Audit, 2000, A sustainable democracy. Politics for popular rule in the 21st century.]. Stockholm: Fritze, (published in the series SOU, 2000:1).

Eriksen, E., and J. Fossum. 2000. *Democracy in the European Union.* London: Routledge.

Esaiasson, P., and K. Heidar. 2000. *Beyond Westminster and Congress: The Nordic Experience*. Columbus: Ohio State University Press.

Esping-Andersen, G. 1990. *The Three Worlds of Welfare Capitalism*. Cambridge: Polity.

Haas, E. 1958. *The Uniting of Europe: Political, Social, and Economic Forces, 1950–1957*. Stanford, CA: Stanford University Press.

Haas, E. 1964. *Beyond the Nation-State: Functionalism and International Organization*. Stanford, CA: Stanford University Press.

Haas, P. 1992. "Introduction: Epistemic Communities and International Policy Coordination." *International Organization* 46 (1): 1–35.

Hanf, K., and B. Soetendorp. 1998. *Adapting to European Integration: Small States and the European Union*. London: Longman.

Jensen, H. 2003. *Europa-udvalget: Et udvalg i folketinget* [The committee of EU Affairs: A committee in the Danish parliament]. Aarhus: Aarhus Universitetsförlag.

Johansson, K. -M. 1999. *Sverige i EU* [Sweden in the EU]. Stockholm: SNS.

Jungar, A. -C. 2009. "The Choice of Parliamentary EU Scrutiny Mechanisms in New EU Member States." In *The European Union and the Baltic States: Changing Forms of Governance*, edited by B. Jacobson, 148–163. London: Routledge.

Jungar, A. -C. forthcoming. "Exporting Nordic parliamentary oversight to the European Union." In *The Promise of Openness: Cultures and Paradoxes*, edited by N. Götz, and C. Marklund.

Karvonen, L. 2004. "Review of Scandinavian Power Studies." *Scandinavian Political Studies* 27 (4): 423–427.

Katzenstein, P. 1985. *Small States in World Markets: Industrial Policy in Europe*. Ithaca, NY: Cornell University Press.

Kurunmäki, J., and J. Strang. 2010. *Rhetorics of Nordic democracy*. Helsinki: Finnish Literature Society.

Makt- og demokratiutredningen [The Audit of Power and Democracy]. 2003. *Makt og demokrati: Sluttrapport fra Makt- og demokratiutredningen* [The final report from the Audit of Power and Democracy]. Oslo: Statens Forvaltningstjeneste (published in the series NOU, 2003:19).

Mény, Y., P. Muller, and J-L. Quermonne. 1996. *Adjusting to Europe: The impact of the European Union on National Institutions and Policies*. London: Routledge.

Miles, L. 1996. *The European Union and the Nordic Countries*. London: Routledge.

Miljan, T. 1977. *The Reluctant Europeans: The Attitudes of the Nordic Countries Towards Europe*. London: Hurst.

Milward, A. 1992. *The European Rescue of the Nation State*. London: Routledge.

Moravcsik, A. 1994. "Why the European Community Strengthens the State: Domestic Politics and International Cooperation." unpublished paper presented at the Conference of Europeanists, Chicago, IL.

Moravcsik, A. 1998. *The Choice for Europe: Social Purpose and State Power from Messina to Maastricht*. London: Routledge.

Olsen, J. P. 2002. "The Many Faces of Europeanization." *Journal of Common Market Studies* 40 (5): 921–952.

Oskarsson, M. 1996. "Skeptiska kvinnor—entusiastiska män. [Sceptical women—enthusiastic men]." In *Ett knappt ja till EU: Väljarna och folkomröstningen 1994* [The voters and the referendum 1994], edited by M. Gilljam, and S. Holmberg, 112–124. Stockholm: Norstedt.

Østerud, Ø., F. Engelstad, and P. Selle. 2003. *Makten og demokratiet: En sluttbok fra Makt- og demokratiutredningen* [Power and Democracy. A final report from the Audit of Power and Democracy]. Oslo: Gyldendal.

Pesonen, P. 1998. "Voting Decisions." In *To Join or not to Join: Three Nordic Referendums on Membership in the European Union*, edited by A. Todal Jenssen, P. Pesonen, and M. Gilljam, 127–146. Oslo: Scandinavian University Press.

Peterson, O. 1994. *The Governance and the Politics of the Nordic Countries*. Stockholm: Fritzes.

Selle, P., and Ø. Østerud. 2006. "The Eroding of Representative Democracy in Norway." *Journal of European Public Policy* 13 (4): 551–568.

Stone Sweet, A., and T. Brunell. 1998. "Constructing a Supranational Constitution: Dispute Resolution and Governance in the European Community." *American Political Science Review* 92: 63–81.

Strandberg, U. 2006. "Introduction: Historical and Theoretical Perspectives on Scandinavian Political Systems." *Journal of European Public Policy* 13 (4): 537–550.

Togeby, L., J. G. Andersen, P. M. Christiansen, T. B. Jørgensen and S. Vallgårda. 2003. *Magt og demokrati i Danmark: Hovedresultater fra Magtudredningen* [Power and democracy in Denmark. The main results from the Power Audit]. Aarhus: Universitetsforlag.

von Sydow, E. 1999. *När Luther kom till Bryssel: Sveriges första år i EU* [When Luther arrived in Brussels: The first years of Sweden in the EU.]. Stockholm: Arena.

'Power Investigation' Neglected: The Case of the Finnish Newspaper *Helsingin Sanomat*

LOTTA LOUNASMERI
University of Helsinki, Finland

ABSTRACT   *A media and communications study conducted within the Finnish research programme on power represents one of the Nordic power investigations. In analysing the discourse of globalisation in the editorials of the largest newspaper of the Nordic countries, Helsingin Sanomat, journalism is studied in one of its most significant societal function: investigating the exercise of power. The understanding of power and those tasked with providing public perspectives on it is seen to be a topic that exceeds the analysis of temporary state commissions. Rather, it concerns the essence of the media system and thus becomes an issue of general relevance.*

The Finnish power investigation known as VALTA, conducted between 2007 and 2010, analysed the political, economic and cultural transformations that Finland had gone through over the previous two decades. The issue was how internationalisation and European integration had affected Finnish power structures, practices and power holders. In one of the projects, devoted to 'Power Elites and Concepts of Power', four researchers examined how key concepts of what they termed the Finnish market regime had been introduced, contested and used in the exercise of societal power.[1] One of the sub-projects, focusing on how the concept of globalisation was apprehended in the editorials of the major Finnish newspaper *Helsingin Sanomat* (HS), at the turn of the current century, is the subject of the present article. The article argues that journalism can be seen as an ongoing power investigation in its ideals and goals, but questions how this goal is achieved. It shows that *HS* uncritically subscribed to the paradigm of economic competition and failed to assume the role of a critical investigator prepared to challenge power, as a modern and vital political culture would have required.

At the turn of the century, globalisation was the subject of much debate in Finland. Internationally, it had become a powerful concept referring to an imagined worldwide societal transformation after the end of the Cold War. Usually globalisation has been connected discursively to the global market system; it has been used to legitimise what is called a competition economy or state.[2] Significant steps towards such a form of economy have been the liberalisation of markets and the subsequent increase in the power of the private business sector. Many explanations have been given for the movement of the Nordic countries towards a competition economy, including the crisis of the welfare state due to its weakening financial base and ideological currents like neoliberalism (Julkunen 2001, 253; Strange 1996). The idea of the competitiveness of a nation is not novel. What is different is the way in which it has been used as an overarching ideology and a discourse in connection with the reforms of the traditionally corporatist Nordic social systems.

Since the 1980s, the exercise of political power and its public legitimation in Finland, along with other European countries and the USA, has been built on the idea of competitiveness (e.g. Kantola and Heiskala 2010). As a part of this discursive power rooted in the ideas of neoliberalism, the role of the nation-state has been defined in a new way: it is now seen increasingly as an efficient machine in international competition for corporate investment, with the logic of productivity permeating all sectors of society. Heiskala and Hämäläinen have listed the characteristics of this new 'mental paradigm' as an appreciation of the market mechanism; the emphasis on competition, innovation and growth; the rise of new technologies; and viewing citizens as consumers (2007, 84–8). These traits, implying openness of the market economy, are also imagined to go hand in hand with political openness and democracy.

In the Finnish context, the changes in the fields of economy and foreign policy have been particularly drastic. A great transition from a corporatism-based planning economy and strict policy of neutrality in the 1960s and 1970s emerged from the 1980s onwards as the country increasingly took part in international competition, and then in 1995, after the collapse of the Soviet Union, joined the European Union. The defeat of 'real socialism' made capitalism as a global economic system grow even stronger (Kettunen 2008, 91).

Finnish mainstream journalism has had an important role in spreading the ideas and vocabulary of the competition economy in recent decades. Concurrently, the motives of Finnish journalism changed, as media companies became increasingly profit-oriented (Luostarinen and Uskali 2006, 179, 189). This development is part of the deconstruction of state interventionism in which market regulation has replaced democratic–corporatist regulation.[3] As a result of journalism being steered more and more by a commercial logic, its traditional ideal of creating a democratic public sphere has been undermined. This is not to say that Finnish media have always succeeded in being a watchdog for democracy in the past. Upholding political stability has often overridden any efforts to question the status quo.

Power in the Public Sphere and Journalism

In classical liberal theory regarding the public sphere, journalism has a special role in facilitating political deliberation and keeping a watchful eye over those in power (Curran 1991, 27–56; Habermas 1990). When a society experiences change and turmoil, such a role becomes even more vital. The ideal role of journalism is a dual one. On the one hand, a normative claim is made to conduct a kind of permanent power investigation through which citizens are continuously informed about its exercise and abuse in their society. On the other hand, some media actors themselves assume the role of spokespersons of the 'common interest' and take as the objective of their work the search for common ground in political life. By doing this they also legitimise existing power structures in society. *Helsingin Sanomat* is a case in point, being the only truly national newspaper in Finland, with a long history of addressing the whole nation and building bridges across the political divide.

As part of their watchdog role in society, journalists are expected to maintain their independence from the powerful elites in society. This is a significant issue, as journalists operate in an inherently contradictory position. Most of the press forms part of the growing private sector of the media economy. Mainstream journalism has a particularly important task in maintaining a balance in its relations with elites so that the press does not simply merge with other leading groups in society. It may well be in the interest of the rulers that the status quo is not shaken by bringing conflicting views into public debate. When elites try to band together and advance a certain political idea or mode of action, swimming against the tide is an essential task for journalism (Asp 1986; Dahlgren 1991; Gibson 2004).

The close, sometimes symbiotic, connections between the press and societal elites are obstacles to a newspaper's, an editor's or a single journalist's practice of independent 'power investigation'. Institutional sources have traditionally been the staple of journalism. Because of this, powerful actors often become the 'primary definers' (Hall et al. 1978) of topics and points of view and influence the language that is used in the public sphere (Heikkilä and Kunelius 1998; Fowler 1991, 22 ff., 118). Recent research has shown that the power and the resources of the public relations sector are growing, while journalistic resources shrink and the competition for news becomes increasingly hectic (Davis 2007).

A substantial academic discussion has been going on about 'mediatisation', a term used to describe the growing influence of media and its logic in different sectors of society (Schulz 2004). Several researchers have concluded that the effects of the media are indirect, that is, it is more of a catalyst than a cause for changes in society. Media exercises power in setting the agenda of the public debate by defining, framing and contextualising events in the daily news. Through this gatekeeper role, the media can affect people's perceptions and interpretations of reality. However, in neither of these respects do the media act independently of other societal actors (Asp 1986; Hallin 1994). The significance of the media is seen as so pervasive that different stakeholders have a strong interest in appearing in the public arena in order to gain legitimacy and to promote their own interpretations of societal development (Lounasmeri 2010, 15 ff.). Väliverronen calls this 'imagined power', as it is built on a belief (a) in the significance of the media, and (b) that all the actors need to adapt to the operational environment shaped by it. Mediatisation not only enhances the influence of the media and the incorporation of media logic in societal practices, he concludes, but is also an interactive process (2012, 91, 95). According to Corner, media power is 'systemic', as it forms just one part of networks of power. This implies that media often lean on elites rather than striving to challenge them (2011, 19). The same conclusion has been reached by others: even if the media have the ability to bring up issues for public discussion, it usually follows the agenda of politicians and decision-making processes, rather than actively creating debate (Davis 2007, 96 ff.; Schudson 2003, 21 ff.).

The role of journalists as critical commentators is especially crucial when powerful actors are like-minded on specific issues, and when these actors' messages are repeated frequently in public. Actively scrutinising and questioning the elites would mean disturbing the general consensus. In a country like Finland, where the elites are traditionally a small group and well connected to each other (Kantola 2002), the media sphere is similarly concentrated and, as mentioned above, there is only one major national newspaper. Views supported by the elite can easily become hegemonic and be promulgated throughout society without questioning, if journalists do not carry out their critical role of identifying and challenging them. In a democracy, creating dialogue and strengthening the voice of civil society is part of the responsibility of journalism. The objective is to create a balance in a society's power relations, which entails treating the representatives of civil society as legitimate participants in public debate.

Newspaper editorials offer political ideas or mental paradigms to their readers—a worldview or angle from which to consider the changing society. Editorials express those shared values or premises upon which parties to a controversy rest their arguments (Alasuutari 1996, 30). A newspaper's acknowledgement of its own discursive power is therefore a precondition for being able to act as a credible investigator of power. Making these premises transparent would be a part of the exercise of rendering societal power visible more generally.

Helsingin Sanomat as a Power Centre of Finnish Media

In the Finnish media scene, power is concentrated in a few large conglomerates with nationwide influence—*Sanoma*, its competitor *Alma Media*, and the public service broadcasting company *YLE*. Kunelius and collaborators who interviewed decision-makers found that the media perception of the Finnish elite was built on a few national news outlets only. To them, *HS* and the television news broadcasts by *YLE* and *MTV3* (part of *Alma Media*) formed the core of the public sphere. Despite the rise of television and the Internet, and the resulting decrease in newspaper circulation, the press was still of importance to power-holders. Decision-makers read *HS* to find out what other members of the elite discussed. The newspaper was also seen as an effective channel for addressing one's peer groups (Kunelius, Noppari, and Reunanen 2009, 265–9). At the same time, *HS* remained an important source of information and a general agenda-setter for other Finnish newspapers, defining what is significant in politics and society even beyond its own readership. Evidently, for a newspaper and media company in such a strong position, it is not uncomplicated to act as a proactive critic of power-holders in society. Given its dominant position in the media landscape, the paper might be expected to take its responsibility as a watchdog over power especially seriously.

Helsingin Sanomat and its predecessor *Päivälehti* have been in the centre of public debate since 1889. Today it is the largest Nordic newspaper with a circulation of 365,994 in 2011.[4] *Sanoma*, the company that publishes *HS*, has become one of the leading media corporations in the Nordic countries and Europe.[5] The paper has a liberal background and supported the National Progressive Party until the 1930s. However, its owners from early on, the Erkko family, developed the paper as a journalistic product, representing the national interest rather than partisan views (see, e.g., Kulha 1989, 118). *Helsingin Sanomat* has, therefore, acted as an instrument of Finnish nation-building and an arena for public discussion, promoting unity and the creation of consensus. In times of societal upheaval, crisis and war, the paper has especially aimed at building bridges between divergent societal groups and has emphasised legality and representative democracy (Juva 1966; Klemola 1981; Kulha 1989; Manninen and Salokangas 2009; Rytkönen 1940, 1946; Tommila and Salokangas 1998). Scholars who have analysed later periods in the paper's existence have noted its endorsement of stable societal development and its shunning of social conflict (Klemola 1981; Lounasmeri 2010, 145–58; Pietilä and Sondermann 1994). The success of *HS* has been traced to its comparatively early disengagement from party politics in favour of bridge-building between the political left and right. It has been a paper for both the bourgeoisie and the working class. In the capital of Finland, *HS* has been 'the paper of the people' since the end of the 1920s, while its main competitor, *Uusi Suomi* (New Finland), remained the paper of the upper class (Tommila and Salokangas 1998, 212–18).

The editorial staff of *HS* has had many connections with the societal elite, especially during the first decades of Finnish independence. The appointment of its editor-in-chief Eljas Erkko as Minister of Foreign Affairs in 1938 brought the paper particularly close to political power. But such connections also prevailed in later periods, resulting in the paper always being well informed about Finnish society and foreign relations (Kulha 1989, 212, 238, 339, 438). A recent study of media and Finnish decision-makers bears witness to the solid connections still prevailing between politicians, leading civil servants, and the principal journalists of *HS*, whom the aforementioned considered members of the elite (Kunelius, Noppari, and Reunanen 2009). As the globalisation debate entered the Finnish public arena in the 1990s, *HS* took it up and suggested a course for navigating the challenge to the nation in accordance with the views of society's most powerful elites.

Editorials Discussing the Challenge of Economic Globalisation

Finland experienced substantial changes with the gradual economic and political opening-up of its society that began in the 1980s. By the 2000s, the global market economy and the European political system reached a new level of integration. The Finnish political elite and the business sector had pushed strongly for neoliberal reforms and the idea of competitiveness. However, at the turn of the millennium, criticism of economic globalisation intensified and massive demonstrations were seen in connection with the meetings of international financial and economic organisations (the World Trade Organisation, G8, the European Union and the World Economic Forum). Globalisation critics who eventually became known as the Global Justice Movement (GJM) felt that business power had grown too strong and democracy had weakened. In Finland the critics also gained a foothold in the public debate because some of the weaker elements of the political elite (MPs from leftist and green parties, the President, and the trade unions) requested greater regulation of trade and more democratic decision making.

Helsingin Sanomat published 1826 articles mentioning the word 'globalisation' between 1992 and 2004 (Lounasmeri 2010, 69; also 69–101 for an analysis of the general globalisation discussion in *HS*). During this time, the concept was discussed in 23 editorials that were written mainly by two contributors, the editor-in-chief Janne Virkkunen, and a member of the editorial team, Antti Blåfield. Their identities were only revealed when the texts were accessed from the paper's in-house archive, not the public online archive, since they did not appear in the newspaper's print editions.

These editorials on globalisation indicate how the paper used its discursive power and related to the tradition of investigating societal power. Discursive analysis was applied to identify the newspaper's linguistic practices: whether there were dominant modes of framing globalisation, and how much space was given to alternative voices and discourse. The way in which the editorials represented and defined the positions of different societal actors and their public messages were also examined. In the tradition of critical discourse analysis, language is seen as constructing reality, in addition to describing it. By analysing language, it is possible to make those constructions, their persistence and modification visible (Fairclough 1992, 41). The objective has been to explain how social reality is continuously constructed, such as in public discussion. When a certain discourse or an idea begins to appear as common sense and gains 'everyone';s' approval, it becomes more difficult to detect or challenge. At this point an idea or ideology takes on the appearance of being hegemonic. Investigative journalism should recognise its own potential to create openness about powerful ideas and also question them when necessary. However, what is found in the editorials of *HS* is a strong tendency to define what it sees as the national interest that needs to be furthered by 'the right kind of politics'. The idea of the competitive nation-state was put forward as the only answer to the challenge of globalisation (see also Kettunen 2008).

When the term globalisation first appeared in public discussions at the end of the 1990s and *HS* was trying to grasp the meaning of the phenomenon, it was typically presented as an independent variable. No discussion was offered about the political decisions leading to the liberalisation of markets and economic globalisation. The editor-in-chief suggested that global economic openness had appeared automatically in connection with technological development, and that democracy would follow as a matter of course:

> Economic globalisation is the consequence of the coming of the knowledge society. It is increasingly easy to disseminate information. This development changes societies from dictatorships to democracies faster than any armies or bombers in the sky. (Virkkunen, *HS*, 16 November 1999)

Editorials on economic globalisation quickly furthered the idea of competitiveness as a way to uphold the national interest and achieve national success. They declared that the people of Finland would have to become competitive in order to succeed in the global economic race. Investing in education was seen as one means to achieve this goal, since the assumption was made that 'a country that does not look after the level of its education does not succeed in the new world' (Virkkunen, *HS*, 16 November 1999). In this connection, market-based solutions were seen as primary answers to the challenges Finnish society faced: the free market would enhance the common good and everyone's wellbeing. As a result, one of the main themes of the globalisation debate was the question of regulating markets. In editorials, regulation was often depicted as protectionism, something with unjust consequences: 'If the borders start closing again, the ones to suffer the most will be the poorest countries' (Blåfield, *HS*, 18 September 1998). Economic openness was deemed the first priority, as something that would maximise utility: 'Building obstacles to world trade is not … the right medication for the problem. On the contrary, the fewer obstacles to world trade, the more people will have the opportunity to share in its benefits' (Blåfield, *HS,* 30 November 1999).

At the same time, the editorials predominantly represented politics as unable to solve the challenges of globalisation. By emphasising the role of the markets, politics became regarded as an area in which people set expectations and hopes, but also as one that was not able to assume an active part in the process of globalisation. The editorials were resigned to the inevitably advancing globalisation: 'Politics still has not demonstrated its ability to contain and rectify the downsides of globalisation. Politics has been a powerless witness to the process of economic globalisation' (Virkkunen, *HS*, 16 November 1999).

Neither did the editorials recognise the power of politics to create the economic openness called 'globalisation', nor to re-regulate the markets. Markets appeared as anonymous and powerful forces, self-referencing and self-regulating, without responsible agents. When the criticism of ordinary people began to appear towards economic globalisation at the turn of the millennium, the editor encouraged politicians to assume a particular role: 'An ungrateful task and a great opportunity for the politicians is to act as a mediator between the viewpoints of the economist and the ordinary citizen' (Blåfield *HS*, 16 April 2000). The change of the economy towards a more market-oriented approach was seen as inevitable, and it was believed that it would spread to all sectors in society. Against this background, the editor granted the politicians some room in which to manoeuvre:

> The task of the politicians is to create rules for the game that enable the necessary reform of the economy but at the same time protect the ordinary citizen.... When economic life is in great turmoil, the rest of society cannot remain static. (Blåfield, *HS*, 16 April 2000)

In 2004, at a later stage in the debate, the editor-in-chief maintained that globalisation had permanently changed societal conditions in the industrialised countries. Thus, the future of Finland as a competitive welfare society would require reform, and the centralised system of collective bargaining in particular (Virkkunen, *HS*, 27 February 2004). This commentary reflected the weakening position of trade unions in the new neoliberal order, although the editorials did not analyse the shift in power relations.

> At such times one should look at the problematics as a whole and also at issues considered untouchable. If one cannot achieve this needed examination of the overall picture, the rigidity on wages will be dismantled in negotiations between the unions. (Virkkunen, *HS*, 27 February 2004)

As globalisation became a theme of domestic politics and was discussed in the context of labour-market relations during 2003 and 2004, the editor-in-chief noted that 'national income policy should not be an end in itself nor an ideological choice'. On the contrary, he pleaded for politics of the 'right kind' that would facilitate the markets:

> The problem of Finnish income policy is that it was built for the conditions of a closed economy ... and we cannot continue the old way. We have to take care of the country's competitiveness by other means .... What is decisive is the substance of the politics that are being exercised; carried out in the right way they will lead towards an industry specific development. (Virkkunen, *HS*, 30 November 2003)

The argument that says politics were necessary as long as they supported the agenda of economic globalisation reveals the hegemonic discourse: the global market economy becomes the absolute value and democratic politics may only serve as an instrument to support policies that enhance competitiveness. *HS* claimed that incomes policy should not be an ideological choice, but at the same time proclaimed that negotiating wages on an industry specific level would be the appropriate way to proceed.

Critics of Globalisation: Well-Meaning But Foolish?

At the turn of the millennium, the globalisation critique presented by the GJM along with Finnish NGOs reached the public arena, and so did the differences of opinion with regard to globalisation and its demands on Finland. This took place especially after parts of the Finnish elite joined in the critique, emphasising the role of politics in solving the problems of globalisation and underlining the plurality of interests in society (see also Lounasmeri and Ylä-Anttila, forthcoming). These groups called for political alternatives and joint responsibility on a global scale. The GJM and other civil society agents were at that time recognised participants in the public debate. But since newspaper editorials emphasised unity and did not recognise genuine conflicts of interest created by globalisation, they presented no other political ideas (or the advocates of those ideas) as equally legitimate to that of the competition state idea and its proponents.

The editorials of *HS* did not hold a high regard for civil society activists, the GJM and NGO representatives. These groups communicated critical views about globalisation politics to a public that could have instead been described by *HS* as an awakening of civil society. However, the paper did not pursue this actively, and the reporting concentrated on describing the demonstrations and other activities as a spectacle. In many editorial comments the civil action was depicted as illegitimate. The paper's editorials emphasised the representative aspects of democracy and saw direct citizen action as undesirable. In connection with the global demonstrations, the editorial section often described criticism of globalisation and its negative effects as an emotional reaction. The views expressed by the demonstrators and NGOs were taken as a sign of people's concern, but not as something that could or should actually affect politics. The editor underlined the significance of rules that would support the weak, but in his view the demonstrators simplified things: 'In the streets of Prague the questions of development become simple slogans. Good is good and bad is bad; there is no grey between black and white' (Blåfield, *HS*, 26 September 2000). Another editor argued for the upsides of globalisation and its ultimate benefits to everyone. He also questioned the legitimacy of the GJM and that of NGOs, and suspected that the protesters failed to understand what they were protesting against:

> Those demonstrating on the streets of Washington want to deny the poor the same method which made them rich themselves; well-meaning but foolish people try to protect the poor from the same development that led to their own prosperity. While doing what they believe to be right, they cause a lot of harm. (Olli Kivinen, *HS*, 20 April 2000)

Elites and the people were depicted as fundamentally different in the editorials: the elites appeared as well-informed, far-sighted, reasonable and acting for the common good, whereas civil society actors or ordinary people were represented as ill-informed, short-sighted, selfish and driven by emotion (see also Büchi 2006, 10 ff.). Commenting on civic action, the editor's statements reveal glimpses of the historically hierarchical character of the Finnish public sphere: educating and civilising the people appeared as the task of the public media (see also Nieminen 2006). At the same time, complaints about the paper's partiality arose: 'The press has not given proper space to the critics nor allowed a proper dialogue' (Misha Dellinger, in a letter to the editors, *HS*, 9 October 2000).

Some of the critical elites and their arguments were challenged during the debate, either directly by *HS* or by sources representing the competition state ideology. When parliamentarians (mostly from the Social Democratic Party, the Left Alliance, and the Greens) sided with the civic movement or made decisions that were in conflict with the market-driven globalisation policies, their judgement was questioned. For example, an editor described the actions of Attac (*Association pour une Taxation des Transactions financières pour l'Aide aux Citoyens* [Association for the Taxation of Financial Transactions and Aid to Citizens]), which established a branch in Finland in 2001, as unrealistic: 'The flavour of defiance comes from the acrimony and idealism of Attac's objectives. Attac wants no less than to control the market forces. So far no one has succeeded in doing this' (Risto Uimonen, *HS*, 2 March 2001).

In the same year, parliament voted 'no' to the sale of the public company Altia (a movement had united people from all sides to stop the sale of this liquor manufacturer of the traditional Finnish Koskenkorva). In the editorial section, parliament's decision was regarded as an emotional reaction. The legitimacy of a democratic decision was certainly acknowledged, but the parliamentarians were not presented as competent representatives of the people:

> Parliament ... has become intoxicated with Koskenkorva.... It seems as if a line of defence has to be drawn somewhere against globalisation: we will not give away our booze factory.... Democracy goes along with slowness.... But one would hope that slowness ... does not mean mental inertia. (Blåfield, *HS*, 11 June 2001)

When the International Labour Organisation (ILO) report prepared by President Tarja Halonen along with the Tanzanian President Benjamin M'kapa, dealing with the social dimensions of globalisation, was published, the editorial section of *HS* saw it as mainly representing 'noble principles'—not to be confused with realistic politics. Nations and their populations should change, the newspaper urged, as their problems were inherently national, and not to be traced back to international markets:

> There are, of course, problems in globalisation development, and there are many fine principles in the report.... A different matter is how well the principles can be fulfilled in practice. Probably not very well.... Very often the problems that have caused a country to be unable to benefit from globalisation are national. (Päivi Isotalus, *HS*, 29 February 2004)

In connection with the issue of globalisation, a lively debate took place in 2004 about the status of the president in Finnish politics. One of the editors suggested that the president had become 'the global conscience'. As economic growth and competition were seen as the prerequisites of development, the issues President Halonen brought forward— sustainable development, cooperation, international solidarity—remained mere hopes (Blåfield, *HS*, 22 September 2004). In the Finnish political system, the president has had considerable authority, and the holder of that office has often exceeded its formal limits by the tacit approval of other organs of government. Those powers were cut significantly after 2000, and the globalisation debate became an element in the renegotiation of the powers of the president. Even this change in the ruling structures and practices in Finland did not provoke analysis in the paper's editorials on globalisation.

National Interest Defines Politics

The editorial section of *HS* did identify differences in the policies of leading politicians on the globalisation question, such as those of President Halonen and Prime Minister Matti Vanhanen (Kivinen, *HS*, 14 December 2004). A solution to the problem this issue posed for the Finnish consensual political system was found in the traditional politics of defending the national interest: 'Instead of embracing the whole world, what is needed is good old style foreign politics—concentrating on those issues most essential to the nation' (Kivinen, *HS*, 14 December 2004).

Searching for political truth and defining the common interest of the nation has been pivotal for the traditional Finnish culture of political debate. This presupposes a belief that a correct solution can be found and that policy measures can be undertaken that rest not on compromise, but on consensus. The role of politics has been to search for and define this consensus. Not much room is left for conflicting views, thereby often legitimising the powers that be. Such a culture was still present in the *HS* editorials. When national interest appears as a common cause, it is also possible to expect the public to work for that goal and make sacrifices for it. When a position is presented as having no alternative, adapting to what seem to be the prevailing conditions becomes the only course of action:

> The slowing down of the growth of the world economy and the simultaneous emergence of globalisation force societies to keep on adjusting and taking care of their success in the tightening competition .... One must simply make it through, and Finland will. (Virkkunen, *HS*, 6 December 1998)

Thus, an immanent crisis was foretold if the nation or the 'people' did not act or adjust accordingly. Government and administration were expected to stand as a united front, discussing challenges without resorting to a plurality of viewpoints:

> Several researchers have warned us of weak signals about Finland's [economic] position .... We must discuss these issues, and the representatives of the state should as well. Messages that contradict each other are not prone to wake people up to prepare for reform, but rather make them falsely confident. (Blåfield, *HS*, 16 October 2004)

The same editor called for national commitment to reforms that should be decided upon unanimously: 'Every year we spend quarrelling among ourselves will make adapting to the great changes in the world economy more difficult' (Blåfield, *HS*, 10 November 2004). As the developments in the world economy were depicted as inevitable, rapid action and reforms were needed in order to avoid a crisis: 'What is now needed is simply political commitment to reforms and change .... Waiting too long will only make the coming decisions harsher' (Blåfield, *HS*, 10 November 2004).

In its editorials discussing economic globalisation, the paper's strongest aspiration was maintaining consensus as it continued to emphasise national interest in the face of an external challenge. The 'common sense' marketed by the paper in its editorials was ideological; it was a political choice made in favour of market-oriented policies and the idea of the competition state. A discourse emphasising political 'realism' and inevitability has also been distinctive in Finnish discussion culture historically, especially when the issue was 'national survival'. This was true in times of war, but also during crises like economic recessions or foreign policy problems. External influences or developments are easily interpreted as threats to the existence of the Finnish nation. National survival and success often seem to be conflated. Kettunen (2008: 60) suggests that historical experiences worked into the 'story of Finland' serve as premises for a discourse of national necessity.

Helsingin Sanomat presented its own position as the only 'reasonable' alternative; other political options were not seen as realistic or viable. This resulted in conflicting views on globalisation being relegated to a less legitimate position, and globalisation itself not being discussed as a genuine societal and political issue. With such an approach, challenging or questioning the existing power structures and individuals in power became of secondary importance to *HS*, and the newspaper neglected its role as a watchdog of power. Legitimising current globalisation policies and elite actors gained a much stronger foothold, and the alternative policy suggestions brought forward by those with less power and influence were not taken seriously.

The idea of a common national interest can be traced back to the early decades of Finnish nation building. There are similarities between *HS*'s editorial style and the so-called Snellmanian discourse. J. V. Snellman (1806–1881) was an influential Finnish statesman and the discursive tradition inspired by his public work has traditionally emphasised representation and disparaged political divisions. Snellman's idea of the state, influenced by Hegel, aimed at a nation with one mind. The nation-state was held together by a moral consensus, he believed, not a pluralistic balance in society (Manninen and Uusitalo 1979, 212). For Snellman, representing the nation did not mean channelling the variable will of the people or individuals, but rather creating the stable will of the nation (Kettunen 2008, 51 ff.). Downplaying societal contradictions, as *HS* did, is in line with Snellman's views, and this tendency can be found in *HS* during the recession of the 1990s as well as the European Union membership debate (Heikkilä 1996, 96f). The secret of *HS*'s long-term success has been its approach of speaking to the people across political boundaries; this seems to have turned into a liability in contemporary society, where the newspaper only talks of what unites the Finns and not what divides them.

Outlook

The traditional role of the media in Finland has been one of stabilising society and keeping morale high, rather than challenging existing power structures and power holders. The history of Finnish political life shows how the dominance of a small elite has marginalised an autonomous journalistic culture and the idea of promoting the interests of citizens through group action instead of via the state apparatus (Herkman 2009). The 'grip' of the political elite only began to loosen during the 1980s as Finnish society became politically, economically and culturally more open and the media more commercialised (Aula 1992; Lounasmeri 2011; Pitkänen 2009). The democratic–corporatist media model has started to crumble, and the country has continued to move towards the liberal model, in which the media break away from political control but depend increasingly on the market (Herkman 2009). In recent years, the Finnish media have taken significant steps to distance themselves from political power. This has been evidenced by the electoral funding crisis that began in 2008, as well as by recent reporting of the Euro crisis. How lasting these changes will be and what their significance for Finnish society will be is still unclear.

Despite these signs of *HS* taking up the task of a watchdog on power, the closeness of the media to political power may have been at least partly replaced by financial ties and goals. These ties will make it difficult to criticise economic agents. Commercialisation is also affecting journalistic practices: there is rarely time to conduct investigative journalism when news must be produced at hyper-speed.

Despite the changing parameters of Finnish journalism, the 'burden' of history and the traditional culture of public discussion still exerts its influence. Consensus-mindedness has its roots in the nation's conflict-filled past and its relation to the neighbouring powers who formerly ruled Finland: Sweden and Russia. Adaptation to externally determined circumstances has played a great role in Finland's political culture, and the public sphere has been used to enhance a common vision of the future of the nation, without much room for dissent. Historically, Finnish journalism has served as an educator and a messenger of the elites, with citizens as addressees rather than participants (Kivikuru 1996, 63). This has often led to journalism that has been unanimous, careful and restrained, suggesting its own objectivity. Such a culture makes politics and political debate seem as though it were governance, rather than a forum for different viewpoints and values. In the present case of public discussion on globalisation, the most recent national objective of uniting the people has been enhancing Finland's competitiveness. Meanwhile, open examination of the actions of those in power, considering the consequences of those actions, and challenging them when necessary, has been all but neglected.

The political cultures of the Scandinavian countries have traditionally emphasised openness, but the structures of power and the individuals who wield it have not been particularly transparent. It is debatable whether the Scandinavian power investigations, despite their apparent transparency and self-analysis, have succeeded in explaining how power works in these societies, or in influencing policymaking and public discussion. They may, in the end, confirm the legitimacy of their governments. Presumably, criticising societal power is especially difficult because the investigator is often too close to the subject. In the relatively small Scandinavian societies, power is often concealed in informal practices and surrounded by silence, as if no one wants to acknowledge its existence or admit possessing it.

For Finnish journalism, and particularly a powerful entity like *HS*, identifying and investigating power is still superseded by legitimising power. Identifying power also applies to identifying one's own position: as a researcher of power should exercise self-reflection, so should a powerful media institution. Having influence in a society places one in a privileged position, and this should be acknowledged by the newspaper. What, then, happens when a media researcher takes up the task of investigating and criticising media power? Altogether neglecting an academic dissertation with a prime focus on a particular newspaper would be difficult in a small country like Finland. The research at hand did arouse the interest of the editor-in-chief of *HS*, Virkkunen, since he attended the researcher's public defence. Still, the official policy line held: the newspaper published a small item reporting on the research, but tempered it by emphasising the paper's policy of providing space for different voices. However, the leftist and anti-establishment paper *Kansan Uutiset* as well as the media professionals' paper *Journalisti*, in articles about the same dissertation, took the opportunity to criticise *HS*—rarely done in Finnish media. In general, self-reflection and criticism arising from within media circles is rare (Davies 2009). Becoming conscious of the power inherent in one's own position would be a first step. In the words of John Stuart Mill: 'Has there ever been power that has not felt natural to those who have possessed it?'

Notes

[1] The researchers were Risto Heiskala from the University of Jyväskylä, and Anu Kantola, Lotta Lounasmeri and Karoliina Malmelin from the University of Helsinki.

[2] See Lounasmeri (2006) for the evolvement of the Finnish public discussion. On the concept of the competition state, see Cerny (1990: 204–47), Kantola (2006) and Heiskala (2006).

[3] Other countries representing the democratic-corporatist model have included the Nordic countries, Germany, Austria and Switzerland. See Hallin and Mancini (2004) and Herkman (2009).

[4] Finnish Audit Bureau of Circulations: www.levikintarkastus.fi/english/statistics.php (accessed 11 December 2012).

[5] Sanoma Oyj has operations in 20 European countries. The group is among the top five European magazine publishers. In addition to Finland, it has a strong position in Belgium, Bulgaria, Croatia, the Czech Republic, Denmark, Estonia, Hungary, Latvia, Lithuania, the Netherlands, Romania, Russia, Serbia, Slovakia, Slovenia and Ukraine. The group has an annual turnover of 2.761 billion Euros and 15,400 employees (2010; Sanoma's annual report 2010.)

References

Alasuutari, P. 1996. *Toinen tasavalta: Suomi 1946–1994* [The Second Republic: Finland 1946–1994]. Tampere: Vastapaino.

Asp, K. 1986. *Mäktiga massmedier. Studier om politisk opinionsbildning* [The Powerful Mass Media. Studies of Political Opinion Building]. Stockholm: Förlaget Akademilitteratur AB.

Aula, M. K. 1992. "Perässä tullaan Amerikka? – Ajatuskoe suomalaisen poliittisen julkisuuden murroksesta." [Following after America? A Thought Experiment on the Finnish Public Sphere] *Tiedotustutkimus* 15 (2): 10–23.

Büchi, R. 2006. *Kohti osallistavaa demokratiaa: Kansanäänestykset demokratian välineenä* [Towards Participatory Democracy: Referenda as Tools of Democracy]. Helsinki: Like.

Cerny, P. G. 1990. *The Changing Architecture of Politics. Structure, Agency and the Future of the State*. London: Sage.

Corner, J. 2011. *Theorizing Media*. Manchester and New York: Manchester University Press.

Curran, J. 1991. *Rethinking the Media as a Public Sphere*. London & New York: Routledge.

Dahlgren, P. 1991. "Introduction." In *Communication and Citizenship: Journalism and the Public Sphere in the New Media Age*, edited by P. Dahlgren, and C. Sparks, 1–24. London: Routledge.

Davies, N. 2009. *Flat Earth News*. London: Vintage Books.

Davis, A. 2007. *The Mediation of Power. A Critical Introduction*. New York: Routledge.

Fairclough, N. 1992. *Discourse and Social Change*. Cambridge: Polity Press.

Fowler, R. 1991. *Language in the News. Discourse and Ideology in the Press*. London & New York: Routledge.

Gibson, T. A. 2004. "Covering the World-Class Downtown: Seattle's Local Media and the Politics of Urban Redevelopment." *Critical Studies in Media Communication* 21 (4): 283–304.

Habermas, J. 1990. *The Structural Transformation of the Public Sphere*. Cambridge: Polity Press.

Hall, S., C. Critcher, T. Jefferson, J. Clarke, and B. Roberts. 1978. *Policing the Crisis: Mugging, the State, and Law and Order*. Basingstoke: Macmillan.

Hallin, D. C. 1994. *We Keep America on Top of the World. Television Journalism and the Public Sphere*. London & New York: Routledge.

Hallin, D., and P. Mancini. 2004. *Comparing Media Systems. Three Models of Media and Politics*. New York: Cambridge University Press.

Heikkilä, H. 1996. "'Teemmepä Kumman Päätöksen tahansa …': EU-keskustelun rakentuminen valtavirtamediassa 1992–1994." ['Whichever Decision We Make…' Construction of the EU discussion in the Mainstream Media 1992–1994] In *Kansa Euromyllyssä* [The People in the Euro Machine], edited by U. Kivikuru, 65–106. Helsinki: Helsinki University Press.

Heikkilä, H., and R. Kunelius. 1998. "Access, Dialogue, Deliberation. Experimenting with Three Concepts of Journalism Criticism." *Nordicom Review* 7 (1): 71–84.

Heiskala, R. 2006. "Kansainvälisen toimintaympäristön muutos Ja suomen yhteiskunnallinen murros." [The Change of the International Environment and the Transformation of the Finnish Society] In *Uusi jako. Miten suomesta tuli kilpailukyky-yhteiskunta* [New Deal. How Finland Became a Competitiveness Society?], edited by R. Heiskala, and E. Luhtakallio, 14–42. Tampere: Gaudeamus.

Heiskala, R., and T. Hämäläinen. 2007. "Social Innovation or Hegemonic Change? Paradigm Change in Finland in the 1980s and 1990s." In *Social Innovations, Institutional Change and Economic Performance*, edited by T. Hämäläinen, and R. Heiskala, 80–94. Cheltenham: Edvard Elgar.

Herkman, J. 2009. "The Structural Transformation of the Democratic Corporatist Model: The Case of Finland." *Javnost – The Public* 16 (4): 73–90.

Julkunen, R. 2001. *Suunnanmuutos. 1990-luvun sosiaalipoliittinen reformi suomessa* [Change of Direction. The Socio-political Reform of the 1990s in Finland]. Tampere: Vastapaino.

Juva, M. 1966. *Suomen kansan historia IV. Kansallinen herääminen* [The History of the Finnish Nation IV: National Awakening]. Helsinki: Otava.

Kantola, A. 2002. *Markkinakuri ja managerivalta. Poliittinen hallinta 1990-luvun talouskriisissä* [Discipline of the Markets and Power of the Managers: Political Governance in the Economic Crisis in Finland in the 1990s]. Tampere: Lokikirjat.

Kantola, A. 2006. "Suomea trimmaamassa: Suomalaisen kilpailuvaltion sanastot." [Trimming Finland: Vocabularies of the Finnish Competition State] In *Uusi jako. Miten suomesta tuli kilpailukyky-yhteiskunta* [New Deal. How Finland Became a Competitiveness Society?], edited by R. Heiskala, and E. Luhtakallio, 156–178. Tampere: Gaudeamus.

Kantola, A., and R. Heiskala. 2010. "Vallan uudet ideat: Hyvinvointivaltion huomasta valmentajavaltion valvontaan." [New Ideas of Power. From the Care of the Welfare State to the Supervision of the Coach State] In *Valta Suomessa* [Power in Finland], edited by P. Pietikäinen, 124–148. Helsinki: Gaudeamus.

Kettunen, P. 2008. *Globalisaatio ja kansallinen me. Kansallisen katseen historiallinen kritiikki* [Globalization and the National Us: Historical Critique of the National Gaze]. Tampere: Vastapaino.

Kivikuru, U. 1996. "Suomalaisen kansalaisyhteiskunnan premissit." [The Premises of the Finnish Civil Society] In *Kansa euromyllyssä* [The People in the Euro Machine], edited by U. Kivikuru, 5–24. Helsinki: Yliopistopaino.

Klemola, P. 1981. *Helsingin sanomat: Sananvapauden monopoli* [Helsingin Sanomat. The Monopoly of Free Speech]. Helsinki: Otava.

Kulha, K. 1989. *Sanasotaa ja sovittelua. Helsingin sanomain poliittinen linja itsenäistymisestä talvisotaan* [War of Words and Reconciliation: The Political Stance of Helsingin Sanomat from Independence to the Winter War]. Helsinki: Sanoma.

Kunelius, R., E. Noppari, and E. Reunanen. 2009. *Media Vallan Verkoissa* (Series A 112/2009, Research Centre for Journalism, University of Tampere).

Lounasmeri, L. 2006. "Globalisaatio helsingin sanomissa: maailmanyhteiskunta vai markkinapaikka?" [Globalization in Helsingin Sanomat: Global Society or a Market Place?] *Ennen & Nyt* 1/2006: 1–18. http://www.ennenjanyt.net/2006_1/lounasmeri.pdf

Lounasmeri, L. 2010. *Kansallisen konsensuskulttuurin jäljillä. globalisaatioajan suomi helsingin sanomissa* [On the Trail of the National Culture of Consensus. Finland in the Age of Globalization in Helsingin Sanomat]. Helsinki: Helsinki University Press.

Lounasmeri, L. 2011. "Sinivalkoisin vai vaaleanpunaisin silmälasein? neuvostoliiton kuva suomalaisessa julkisuudessa tshekkoslovakian miehityksestä janajevin junttaan." In *Näin Naapurista. Median Ja Kansalaisten Venäjä-Kuvat*, edited by L. Lounasmeri, 68–124. Tampere: Vastapaino.

Lounasmeri, L., and T. Ylä-Anttila. forthcoming. "Ruptures in National Consensus: Economic versus Political Openness in the Globalization Debate in Finland." In *The Promise of Openness. Cultures and Paradoxes*, edited by N. Götz, and C. Marklund. Leiden: Brill.

Luostarinen, H., and T. Uskali. 2006. "Suomalainen journalismi ja yhteiskunnan muutos." In *Uusi jako. miten suomesta tuli kilpailukyky-yhteiskunta?* edited by R. Heiskala, and E. Luhtakallio, 179–201. Helsinki: Gaudeamus.

Manninen, O., and R. Salokangas. 2009. *Eljas erkko. Vaikenematon valtiomahti* [Eljas Erkko. The State Power That Did Not Stay Silent]. Helsinki: WSOY.

Manninen, J., and J. Uusitalo. 1979. "J.V. Snellmanin vuoden 1840 kirjoitukset valtiosääntöuudistuksen periaatteista." [The 1840 Writings of J.V. Snellman about the Principles of the Constitution Reform] In *Aate ja maailmankuva. Suomen filosofista perintöä keskiajalta vuosisadallemme* [Ideology and Worldview. The Philosophical Legacy of Finland from the Middle Ages to Our Century], edited by S. Knuuttila, J. Manninen, and I. Niiniluoto, 174–231. Porvoo: WSOY.

Nieminen, H. 2006. *Kansa seisoi loitompana. Kansallisen julkisuuden rakentuminen suomessa 1809–1917* [The People Stood Further Away: the Construction of the National Public Sphere in Finland 1809–1917]. Tampere: Vastapaino.

Pietilä, V., and K. Sondermann. 1994. *Sanomalehden yhteiskunta* [Society of the Newspaper]. Tampere: Vastapaino.

Pitkänen, V. 2009. "Politiikan journalismin yhteiskunnallinen tehtävä." [The Task of Political Journalism in Society] In *Politiikan journalismin tila suomessa* [The State of Political Journalism in Finland], edited by V. Pernaa, M. K. Niemi, and V. Pitkänen, 79–108. Turku: Kirja-Aurora.

Rytkönen, A. 1940. *Päivälehden historia I. 1880-luvun 'nuoret' ja päivälehden perustaminen* [History of Päivälehti I. The 'Youth' of the 1880s and the founding of Päivälehti]. Helsinki: Sanoma Oy.

Rytkönen, A. 1946. *Päivälehden historia II. päivälehden ulkonaiset puitteet ja kirjalliset profiilit* [History of Päivälehti II. The External Conditions and Literary Profiles of Päivälehti]. Helsinki: Sanoma Oy.

Schudson, M. 2003. *The Sociology of News*. New York & London: W.W. Norton & Company.

Schulz, W. 2004. "Reconstructing Mediatization as an Analytical Concept." *European Journal of Communication* 19 (1): 87–101.

Strange, S. 1996. *The Retreat of the State: The Diffusion of Power in the World Economy*. Cambridge: Cambridge University Press.

Tommila, P., and R. Salokangas. 1998. *Sanomia kaikille. Suomen lehdistön historia* [News to Everyone. The History of the Finnish Press]. Helsinki: Edita.

Väliverronen, E. 2012. "Median kuviteltu valta." In *Julkisuus ja demokratia* [The Imagined Power of the Media], edited by K. Karppinen, and J. Matikainen, 83–105. Tampere: Vastapaino.

Power and Society in Finland: Change and Continuity

AINUR ELMGREN

University of Helsinki, Finland

ABSTRACT   *Unlike its sister investigations in Norway, Sweden and Denmark, VALTA, the Finnish research programme on power, conducted from 2007 to 2010, was not directly commissioned by the state, but by the Academy of Finland. It claimed a more independent approach, both theoretically and methodically, than TANDEM, a thematically similar research programme in the 1970s. This article analyses the narratives constructed to advertise the VALTA programme and present its results to the public. It also examines how the key concepts of the programme, power and citizenship, were influenced by the views on historical change expressed by the investigators. In the framing narratives of the investigation and several of its individual projects, such change was defined as a displacement of the welfare state by a new model, one in which the state served as a coach for its citizens in a climate of heightening economic competition. Passive images of the citizen and the sometimes contradictory historical narratives contained in the framing articles obscured the results of the individual projects, which often uncovered civic agency in the uses of power in society.*

The Academy of Finland financed a multi-disciplinary research programme from 2007 to 2010 with the full title 'Valta Suomessa—Power in Finland', henceforth referred to as VALTA. The programme's individual studies covered a variety of subjects, a selection of which was presented in an anthology also entitled *Valta Suomessa*. This anthology and the project's final report, both published in 2010, as well as the programme memorandum of 2005 and the evaluation report of 2012, are here analysed from three complementary perspectives. First, the national narrative that was used to package and explain the significance of VALTA to decision-makers and the wider public is scrutinized. Then, views on limits and potentials of power within the VALTA project are compared. Finally, expectations of the VALTA programme as expressed in the following public debate, including those voiced after the fact in the evaluation report of 2012, are explored. This examination considers how VALTA has been marketed to a specialist audience and to the general public, and why—and in which ways—it was expected to influence the public discourse on power.

While the individual sub-projects of VALTA have produced numerous independent publications, the anthology was the only common one issued by the programme. It was a showcase for both the whole programme and selected sub-projects. However, as revealed at the VALTA evaluation report seminar in Helsinki organised by the Academy of Finland on 23 April 2012, the anthology was also used to promote the results of the project to decision-makers, indicating it was a significant part of the media strategy of VALTA. The other publications, including the 2005 memorandum, the 2010 report, and the 2012 evaluation, are not as extensive in scope. All are accessible on the website of the Academy of Finland and provide information about the motives and expectations of the programme.[1]

Unlike other Scandinavian public investigations on power, the VALTA programme was not commissioned by the state. The 2005 programme memorandum characterised the VALTA initiative as in the tradition of the Nordic power investigations, but presented a truncated version of their history. According to the memorandum, the Nordic investigations responded to the same challenges that Finland was facing. 'Globalisation, the EU's increasing decision-making power, individualisation, commercialisation, the increased role of international justice obligations and the legal sector' were depicted as challenging democracy and traditional power structures in all Nordic countries (Akatemia 2005, 52). Other factors portrayed as equally urgent included multiculturalism, the media, the environment and technological development. The historical overview of power investigations was limited to the 1990s. Sweden was mentioned as the initiator of several power enquiries, yet the ground-breaking role of Norway was ignored in the memorandum. It also noted that Finland had not conducted any comparable investigation on power and democracy before. However, in the *Valta Suomessa* anthology, the Nordic power investigations were not mentioned. Instead, the introduction referred to a previous scholarly investigation on power and democracy in Finland, TANDEM (Research on Equality and Democracy 1977), as its predecessor (Pietikäinen 2010a).

According to the memorandum, the main goals of VALTA were the support and advancement of high-level research collaboration and multidisciplinary studies, international mobility, and the application and development of new research methods. The programme was also meant to conduct comparative research on power in Finland, thus clarifying the specific characteristics of the country's power structures and power mechanisms, and giving thought to their similarities and differences in relation to other countries and cultures. It is less clear whether any preparatory or deliberative function of VALTA was intended in the sense that historian Edenheim (2010) defines the specific task of the Swedish public investigation. It was not a stated purpose of VALTA to provide long-term policy guidelines for social and legal change, which Edenheim calls 'the preparatory function' (2010, 35). However, the concluding goal in the memorandum stated that the programme aimed to improve the exchange of information and reporting of research results among scholars, decision makers, interest groups and the public at large, and influence the public debate on power in Finland.

The preparatory function is of particular interest here. The public discourse produced by VALTA researchers and the media during the two years after the programme ended (2010–2012) did not consider VALTA itself as a tool for the exercise of power in a preparatory sense. However, the material published by the Academy of Finland showed VALTA's intention to exercise power by taking on a deliberative function in public debate. In the 2005 memorandum, the other Nordic power investigations were characterised as having produced new knowledge and inspired 'both national and international debate' (Akatemia, 2005, 52). Opportunities for comparative perspectives were opened up by the results, and the memorandum mentioned that Finland had thus far not produced anything comparable. It concluded that a Finnish power study would both relate to previous Nordic experiences and generate new information about specific national features of power structures. The impression was that the ground-breaking policy changes in Finland had been enacted 'without an extensive political debate', which further increased the urgency of a comprehensive analysis (Akatemia 2005, 54). However, there were hopes to improve the communication between different interest groups and societal actors and influence public debate by supplying arguments based on the work of experts, akin to 'the deliberative function' of the Swedish power investigation.

Despite being the last in a list of six 'main goals', this point received much attention in the final external evaluation of VALTA commissioned by the Academy of Finland and published in 2012. The report was based on the researchers' self-reports, interviews with 'key persons' in the programme and media analysis prepared by the Academy of Finland Communications Unit. The report noted the weak coverage in the media, despite the whole programme's attempt to engage the public. Media interest tended to focus on specific projects connected with current policy debates (Evaluation panel 2012). The evaluation was also concerned with the preparatory function of the research results, although the programme memorandum had not expressed such a goal in 2005. The anthology, the main target of analysis in this article, was 'widely distributed among policymakers' (select members of parliament, according to speakers at the evaluation report seminar in Helsinki), but there was no evidence the book had any impact on legislative processes or debates about policy decisions. The report concluded that it was 'difficult to judge (or measure) the exact nature of the programme's impact on policymakers'. This was not surprising, given the weak emphasis on this goal in the programme memorandum and the lack of interpretations indicating political uses of the results in the programme publications. Nevertheless, the conclusion generated concerned debate during the seminar. It was believed that specific projects did have an impact on a 'general debate about policy-relevant matters', although the report did not specify how the evaluation team had reached this conclusion and no concrete examples were given (Evaluation panel 2012, 20–1).

Despite its analysis of societal change, crisis and topical issues of the day, VALTA struggled with public outreach, as evidenced by the lively discussions during the evaluation seminar. Speakers representing the Academy of Finland defended the programme's independence from political agenda setters, while speakers representing individual projects and external commentators lamented the lack of political interest in the results.[2]

The Long Shadow of TANDEM

Although VALTA was a new and ground-breaking programme in Finland, the documents it produced and some of the scholarly reviews it received referred to an earlier research programme that made history in the development of the social sciences in Finland and had succeeded in creating a heated public debate. Inspired by the Scandinavian power investigations, VALTA has been compared to the 1970s TANDEM study, a research programme dominated by social scientists (Gronow, Klemola, and Partanen 1977). For example, VALTA was contrasted with TANDEM by programme coordinator Petteri Pietikäinen in his preface to *Valta Suomessa*. In Pietikäinen's reading, the final TANDEM report, despite its dismal picture of Finland in the 1970s, promised a better future. As he saw it, the difference was that nowadays few researchers believed in revolution or benevolent power, and Marxist theory had been dethroned by the combating schools of Foucauldian constructivism and 'ontological realism' (Pietikäinen 2010a, 10).[3]

In a summary essay on the website of the Academy of Finland posted after the conclusion of the programme, Pietikäinen declared that VALTA was unique, even from an international perspective, because it was a multidisciplinary research programme. 'I do not know of any corresponding multi-voiced research programme on power anywhere else in Europe, least of all in Scandinavia' (Pietikäinen 2010d, 1). The general results, he explained, confirmed that power in Finland had changed in character since the 1970s and 1980s. The choice of a point of reference in time pointed implicitly to TANDEM because the actual VALTA results had dealt with a much longer time-frame. Pietikäinen also stated that the researchers often appeared in media and that this must have led to an increase in civic debate on power and powerlessness. He later appeared in the media and expressed a pessimistic opinion of citizens uninterested in taking power into their own hands (Anonymous 2013).

Pietikäinen might have felt the need to distance the programme ideologically from TANDEM. Sociologist Sulkunen (2010) has even referred to a 'TANDEM trauma' in his review of the VALTA anthology. TANDEM has been strongly criticised for having its theoretical basis in a Marxist analysis of class and the production system rooted in historical materialism. Moreover, 'Marxism' in Pietikäinen's text refers to a political programme rather than a sociological theory: 'Unlike today's researchers, the makers of the TANDEM programme did not see power in itself as a problem. Their problem was that power rested in the wrong hands' (Pietikäinen 2010a, 9). Marxist-inspired analysis was a novelty in the social sciences in Finland at the time, and much of the resistance to TANDEM mirrors the broader political conflicts in the country during the 1970s (Leimu 1977). The reception of TANDEM has been characterised as hostile, but as a media strategy, the conflict-oriented approach delivered impressive results. The programme had a recurring presence in the headlines for some years before the publication of the final report. Among its critics, TANDEM could count renowned scholars and politicians, leading publicists and even popular cartoonists. During the final year of the investigation, it inspired an aggressively worded pamphlet against a specific sub-project presented to the Minister of Education by the Research Foundation for Higher Learning and Science Politics (Korkeakoulu- ja Tiedepoliittinen Tutkimussäätiö, KTTS), and an entire book that included some very harsh refutations of the results and methods of the entire programme (Rautkallio and Häikiö 1977; Vesikansa 1976). The debate became heated to such an extent that the respected non-Marxist philosopher Georg Henrik von Wright made a public statement on behalf of the freedom of science and research, defending the TANDEM scholars against their detractors (see Toiviainen 1977).

Former TANDEM investigator Partanen (1992) described the public discourse on TANDEM as partly instigated by the Finnish Business and Policy Forum (EVA) and the aforementioned KTTS. Both institutions were founded in the 1970s to counter a perceived leftist turn in the Finnish media and political sphere (Mäkinen 2002; Toiviainen 1977). However, other researchers have maintained that an equally important role was played by the press eager to uncover waste of money and combat 'zero-research', a term used to denounce the provocative methods and goals of the TANDEM investigation (Leimu 1977, 236, footnote 48). Partanen considered the long-term significance of TANDEM as deserving of more than the tumultuous reception it received in some quarters. However, the scandal remained a point of reference in Finnish social science, and it influenced the framing narrative of VALTA.

A broad and multidisciplinary research programme in the humanities and social sciences can be made accessible to a non-specialist audience by embedding it in historical narratives about the nation and the development of society. Since individual TANDEM sub-projects contradicted established narratives on the past, the programme as a whole was defended with references to the national interest. When Pekka Sulkunen reviewed the TANDEM report in 1977, he stated that, despite his own critical reading, the 'concern for our future as a nation touches also those who find scientific Marxism alien'. Moreover, he acknowledged that TANDEM revealed the contradictions within the economic structure that shaped the nation's future. The conflicts arising from these contradictions ought to be combated by a 'determined people' because 'the democratic alternative is simultaneously a question of national self-esteem' (Sulkunen 1977, 64–8). Sulkunen's interpretation made Marxist analysis palatable to the general public by appealing to the national narrative of a united people with a common cause.

The national focus also appeared strongly in the public discourse on VALTA. Reviewers of the *Valta Suomessa* anthology were more interested in the VALTA programme's connections to TANDEM than to the Scandinavian power investigations, despite Pietikäinen's attempts to prove VALTA's independent position in his introduction to the anthology. Both Sulkunen (2010) and social scientist Saari (2010) claimed that TANDEM in some ways predicted the processes studied by VALTA, and that some of the articles in the anthology voiced stronger criticism of the market ideology of economic growth than the TANDEM report had ever done. Despite this radicalism, the reviewers did not expect a public reaction similar to the TANDEM controversy. Sulkunen speculated that the need to distance VALTA from TANDEM in Pietikäinen's contribution to the anthology might have arisen from a methodological resistance to 'society' as an object for research (perhaps hinting at the comparatively humble role of sociological research within the VALTA programme). According to Sulkunen, an article by Risto Heiskala and Anu Kantola on the transformation of the welfare state into a 'coach state' was closest to the TANDEM approach. While positively received by other social scientists, the article ignited a brief debate in the leading newspaper *Helsingin Sanomat*, in which a contributor interpreted it as an anachronistic call to return to the high tax rates of the 1970s, faintly echoing the TANDEM furore (Hämäläinen 2010; Heiskala and Kantola 2010b; Ojala 2010).

The VALTA Anthology and Its Main Themes

The final report of the VALTA programme included 22 different projects, 10 of which were represented by articles in the *Valta Suomessa* anthology (see Pietikäinen 2010c). The volume also included the preface and a concluding article by Petteri Pietikäinen and a historical essay by Pertti Haapala. These provided an informal context that also served as a framing structure for the anthology. The contents were divided into three sections, the first of which bore a complicated pun in its heading: 'Valta virtaa' (Power Is Streaming/ Flowing, but alternatively reading 'valtavirtaa'—mainstream). Under this heading, articles dealing with temporal changes and processes were collected, such as changes in the structure of societal elites and in the economic structure of Finland. In the second section, 'Vallan oikeuttaminen' (Justification/Legitimation of Power), articles dealt with different ideal types of citizens and civic action, as well as the self-image of city planners and the legitimation of uses of power on the local level. The third section, 'Valta ja kansalaiset' (Power and the Citizens) contained a variety of studies on leadership methods with analyses on how citizenship was produced by the media.

It is unclear on what basis some sub-projects provided articles to the anthology and others did not. VALTA included several projects on gender issues, but only one was featured in the anthology. A number of projects on power in economics of the public sector and in public institutions were omitted, as well as perspectives on the ageing population, immigration, power in the justice system, and the European Union. There may have been pragmatic reasons for this decision, since projects were not necessarily concluded in time to be included in the anthology.

The idea of 'increasing individualisation' appears in a few of the anthology articles, although it is contradicted by the steady public support for welfare policies, and the decline (or persistent absence) of support for political parties claiming to represent the new individualist citizen-consumer. Some studies tend to confirm the hegemony of individualisation; others point to the continuity of collective identification. Numerous project summaries in the anthology and online documentation address this paradox only in passing or not at all. One cannot expect uniformity from a power investigation with such a large scope and broad ambitions. Still, attempts to explain the purpose of the project as a reaction to a pivotal shift from collective to individualised civic identification appear in both the framing chapters and some of the articles on individual projects.

Another concern is the concept of accountability that sporadically appears in the anthology. Openness is not only a top-down process of voluntary concession by those in power, or simply compliance with existing laws. It can also be demanded or enforced by citizen groups that take collective action on behalf of various causes. The concept of accountability in the Finnish context is closely related to perceptions of past and future change. In many of the articles, the concept of power, while acknowledged to be fluid and horizontal as well as hierarchical, appears as a rigid top-down process that follows historically determined paths. The project , Petteri Pietikäinen, posed a series of unanswered questions to express the need for future research on power. He wondered what freedom of movement was left to the individualist citizen-consumer, how the activist-citizen could find the means to organise, and how power relations could be changed. Pietikäinen's concluding words were both a call to scholars and a normative claim for the common task of citizens: 'When it is a citizen's virtue to be an enlightened watchdog of power, Finland will be more distinctly a civilised nation' (2010d, 1). Virtuous citizens are portrayed as needing to take action, but it remains unclear by what means they can become engaged. Pietikäinen's optimistic note fits the narrative purpose of his article, providing a satisfying conclusion to the VALTA project by pointing towards a brighter future and encouraging further scholarly work on the subject.

Despite its optimistic view, Pietikäinen's statement can also be interpreted as a disillusioned comment on the present. In 1992, TANDEM researcher Juha Partanen, looking back on the 1970s project, commented that, from the perspective of developing democracy, the concluding TANDEM report was gloomy reading. The project's starting point was the idea of democracy as rational collaboration rather than adherence to formal principles and state institutions. However, the project found little civic activism that would have fulfilled this expectation. Among the problems were the priority of foreign relations in Finnish policy-making, 'monopoly capitalism', historically limited opportunities to enact societal reforms, corporatism and ideological control, yet TANDEM did not propose any concrete solutions or identify who would enact such policies. As described by

Partanen, they could only perceive a gradual limitation of democracy. In his opinion, the 1980s had not brought much positive change, except for some release from external pressure as a result of the end of the Cold War, and he assumed the transfer of power to Brussels might change that, too (Partanen 1992, 198).

The VALTA memorandum explained the need for power research by numerous references to change, especially contrasting a past marked by continuity, a present marked by ruptures, and a future that would bring numerous challenges and threats (Akatemia 2005, 53). Its alarmist image of the future was understandably designed to make the project proposal attractive, although seen from a historical perspective these incentives and threats were also present 15 years previously—not to speak of the energy crisis and environmental movement of the 1970s, the rise of youth culture and political activism in the 1960s, or the numerous political and economic crises before and after the Second World War. TANDEM participant Partanen (1992, 194) described the early 1970s as a time when 'many felt that anything was possible', and 'Finnish society was in a state of dramatic change'—a positive view of change that nevertheless might have resonated with crisis-struck readers in the early 1990s.

According to Pietikäinen, the VALTA investigators had a normative interest in redefining the role of the citizen. Instead of being obedient subjects and following established customs, citizens were expected actively to hold accountable those who exercise public power: 'perhaps power researchers in the future will confirm that power in Finland is transparent and increasingly in the hands of aware and enlightened citizens' (Pietikäinen 2010b, 259). Considering the fact that the programme memorandum defined democracy as civic participation and civic power, it is surprising that Pietikäinen's conclusion in the anthology imagined that citizens taking an active role would become a reality in the future, not something that already existed in the present (Akatemia 2005, 58). The influence of the VALTA programme in a wider societal and political context also remains vaguely formulated in the framing articles, in comparison to the goals set up in the programme memorandum of 2005. There had been opportunities to respond to outside expectations; during the research period, calls to study change were raised in social science publications and directed at the research community in general (Kortteinen 2008). The evaluation report, in contrast to the anthology's framing articles, gave the impression that the programme was expected to have an impact on policymaking and public opinion and in this way perhaps serve the cause of openness and transparency. The evaluation report also expressed dissatisfaction with the lack of public debate occasioned by the programme.

Perhaps the wording of the programme's conclusion was purposefully tentative. Instead of taking a proactive stance and describing active citizens already participating on different levels in the exercise of power, the presumed actual role of the citizen emphasised passivity and the reception of ideas conveyed by elite-dominated media and policymaking. The first section of the anthology focused on elite groups and changes in hierarchies and showed how collective action had been a more or less conscious strategy for those who professed an ideology of individualist competition (Kallioinen et al. 2010). From 1939 to 1944, the war prompted cartel leaders to accept state-led economic planning, something that paradoxically went along with an increase in the rhetorical praise of competition. In the texts and speeches produced by cartel leaders and business owners at the time, competitiveness was praised as an essential trait of the individual Finn and Finns as a collective, as a guarantee of individuality, success and Finnish nationhood. The emphasis in such articles was on power exercised either by a dominant, privileged group, or by a subordinate group navigating within norms that kept it subordinated. There was not much room to rethink the citizen's role within this historical framework.

The notion of the post-modern individual as independent of traditional or modern communities and interest groups appears in the second and third sections of the anthology. Heiskala and Kantola (2010a) claim that a 'coach state' has supplanted the welfare state, and this coach state generates postmodern individualists as citizens. The related concept of the citizen-consumer appears in the chapter on energy politics (Ruostetsaari 2010, 178) and in two articles with a structural critique on media production of citizenship and the 'ideal subject' (Jääsaari et al., 2010, 223; Lehtonen and Koivunen, 2010, 241). Heiskala and Kantola diversify the concept of the citizen with several models of individualism. They expand the neo-liberal image of citizen-consumers to people who 'break apart from traditional trade hierarchies, social groups and parties, and see themselves more and more as individuals, whose lives are no longer dictated by institutions' (Heiskala and Kantola 2010a, 148). This analysis is placed in a historical context and compared with traditional Hegelian–Lutheran individualism, rooted in common moral principles that enabled the creation of the modern welfare state. However, the new individualisation of the urban middle class is seen as not just self-interested, but 'a liberating and inspiring force' in society, beyond the confines of the market. The authors suggest that future policymaking must have the interest of this group in mind, yet they offer no clear description of the possibilities of this group acting as a political subject (Heiskala and Kantola, 2010a, 148). Ruostetsaari (2010, 188) warns in an article on the citizen-consumer and energy politics that the ability to stay informed on the implications of one's choices is limited, and that the ability to vote with one's wallet hardly constitutes a democratic process.

It remains unclear how this citizen-consumer is related to the ideological concept 'citizen-consumer' coined by New Labour in 1998 and cited by Lehtonen and Koivunen (2010, 242). Quite a few of the authors do not distinguish between the analytical term and the ideological variant. Jääsaari and co-authors (2010, 226) translate the English neologism 'prosumer' as *tuluttaja* (from *tuottaja* + *kuluttaja*, producer + consumer) to emphasise the active role of the citizen-consumer, but they simultaneously hold that citizen activism in the so-called new media involves collective mobilisation and organisation. Studies showing citizens doubt that they have the ability to influence the media contradict this optimistic neologism. The authors insist on the individualism of the prosumer, although they admit that collective strategies of political action are still powerful, citing the Pirate Party as an example, though ignoring a more influential political party, the True Finns (2010, 228). Klaus Helkama's research team, in their project 'Power in Finland's Forestry and Environmental Policy as Conceived by Citizens', also found that citizens were themselves actively engaged in local causes (Helkama et al., 2010). Kimmo Lapintie's (2010) article on the role of architects in city planning and development contained a discussion on concepts of power that would fit well in an introductory chapter.

The concluding article by Mikko Lehtonen and Anu Koivunen (2010) raises the issue of the success of populist politicians in contrast to individualist self-interest promoted by consumer culture and policymaking designed to keep the citizens passive. The authors point out that the ideal middle-class 'we' produced by mainstream culture is based on exclusion, and that populist politicians might use this to prove how 'the people's voice' is silenced or distorted. New citizen-consumers are seen as free to choose how and why to exercise their power, but at the cost of an increasingly large segment of the population with fewer resources and opportunities. The same authors subsequently edited an anthology of their own, *Kuinka meitä kutsutaan?* (Koivunen and Lehtonen, 2011), which developed their sub-project with other scholarly contributions and functioned as the kind of interdisciplinary collaboration that was requested by the 2005 memorandum. Curiously, the editors of *Kuinka meitä kutsutaan?* fail to mention that their sub-project, PowCult, belonged to VALTA. In analysing power relations, the anthology concentrates on agency, although Lehtonen's and Koivunen's topic in *Valta Suomessa* concerned ideological struggles in the public sphere. The focus on agency—belonging to actual individuals and agenda setters, or to interest groups—avoids the confines of a narrative adhering to national and historical stereotypes.

Valta Suomessa did not attempt to represent the whole scope of VALTA, nor did it aim at a particular subject covered by the programme. As such, it is not directly comparable to this specialised anthology. Of all the articles included, only one dealt with environmental politics, although many of its contributors describe environmental and climate-related issues as urgent challenges (Helkama et al., 2010). No article dealt with the increasingly conflicted topics of immigration, refugee politics, multiculturalism, or development collaboration, although these topics were presented as challenges for Finland in the near future. Sub-projects pertaining to immigration issues and minority politics have been collected in an anthology, which, as of 2013, had not yet been published (Kivistö and Kraus forthcoming). While immigration questions have received much attention in the national media and had made an impact on the 2011 parliamentary election campaign, research dealing with these issues was directed at an international audience, not the Finnish-speaking public. This was probably the result of a scholarly publication strategy rather than an attempt to avoid the topic in domestic debate. Nevertheless, the anthology missed some themes that might have aroused the interest of the media or certain politicians who were provided with their own copy.

The National Narrative and Civic Agency

As an overview of a multifaceted programme, the anthology's collection of studies showed certain disparities. The memorandum, the preface, the afterword and the ensuing debates created a framework for the whole investigation, namely the history of the nation-state of Finland, demarcated by events representing change. This resembles the ideological framework of the TANDEM programme, described as a project triggered by pivotal change in the notion of a national historical continuum. The difference consists of the narratives used to legitimise the programme to the public. In these narratives, the perceptions of the ideal versus the actual citizen were influenced by notions of historical change. The studies themselves focused not on the citizens' power to change their situation, but rather on the elusive power structures themselves, which trapped the citizens in subjective experiences that enticed them to accept the roles that they were offered (consumerist, heterosexual, middle-class, moral majority, etc.). Pietikäinen's (2010a, 17) preface embedded the VALTA programme in a framing narrative in which any personified subjects were absent: 'For the purposes of the production of consent it is important that the publicly constructed ideal "we" evokes desire to identify and belong'. The question of who is doing the constructing is left for others to answer. The notion of power as practices that seemingly generate themselves is nothing new, but the author's reluctance to identify those who profit from it, as well as those who resist it or subvert it, cannot simply be explained as a division of labour between those investigators that were studying power as a resource and others studying structural power.

Some scholars did not hesitate to identify the ideological motivations of specific power relations. Kalela (2008) cited a political elite that adopted the media's image of citizens as passive targets for policymaking with the concerns of egoistic consumers. In the VALTA programme, Kimmo Lapintie, who studied self-legitimation among city planners, revealed how certain kinds of knowledge are more highly valued than others, and why. He warns of the consequences for a changing society, but the agents for change remain abstract:

> certain fields of knowledge, e.g. more exact information about immigrants, may remain out of reach for a longer time. Most likely, they will not receive attention until societal pressure has grown strong enough. At that point, Finnish welfare state planning will probably have to reflect on how outdated its own teachings are. (Lapintie, 2010, 123)

The VALTA investigation may also have to consider whether its teachings will become obsolete in the near future. The framing articles by Petteri Pietikäinen and Pertti Haapala, as well as some of the thematic articles, endorsed stereotypical narratives of the nation, despite presenting new analyses. The study on continuities in elite formations by Ruuskanen, Snellman and, Widgren, showed how Finland as an autonomous grand duchy in the Russian Empire was led by a class of noblemen-officials up to the 1880s, with education gradually replacing estate as the determining recruitment factor. The egalitarian Finland 'as we know it' is the relatively recent result of such processes. Nevertheless, the article concludes: 'Finland is a small country, where everyone knows each other. Therefore, societal differentiation is limited and there are no great gaps between different social groups' (Ruuskanen, Snellman, and Widgrén, 2010, 54). On the basis of the interviews conducted within the project, the article claims that Finland's decision-makers do not view themselves as belonging to an elite. However, generalising statements based on the self-description of groups cannot be of equal value as empirical proof of inequality. The authors describe the hesitation to self-identify with a privileged group as a Finnish characteristic and see increases in inequality, such as the growth of income gaps and accelerating multiculturalism, as a future problem, unrelated to similar experiences in the past. This simplistic narrative has been endorsed and criticised in the past, and it has not gone unchallenged in modern Finnish historiography (Loima, 2006). The hegemonic narrative of the homogeneous nation contradicts historical knowledge and empirical evidence, but provides a recognizable point of reference to a popular audience.

A sub-project referred to in the concluding chapter not directly represented in the anthology describes another social change in support of the discourse on individualism and the 'prosumer' (Pietikäinen, 2010b, 256). Lauri Karvonen studies the change in Finnish politics as it moved from a class-based party democracy to an 'audience democracy', in which situation-dependent lifestyle choices determine political identification. Karvonen's team's experimental study on participants in a citizen forum debating nuclear power seemed to confirm this theory, according to their analysis. However, the study found that the participants strongly identified with their local communities rather than with global lifestyles. The image presented of the participants seemed both to confirm and contradict the individualisation model, but Pietikäinen chose to focus on the results that supported the model of an audience democracy in which passive consumers lacked strong group identities. Other studies have produced similarly contradictory results. An examination of political behaviour of the Swedish-speaking minority in Finland revealed that trust in experts remained high, but people also wanted to develop methods of direct democracy instead of relying on representative institutions (Bengtsson and Mattila, 2011). What is described as a break with traditional collective identification can also be interpreted as the formation of new collective interest groups.

Whereas other forms of public power follow the predicted course—party programmes and political leadership giving way to media-savvy image specialists and public power converging with private interests and the financial market—the individual citizen insists on seeing the world through the local collective's eyes. Perhaps we may find here the cause that mobilises so-called citizen-consumers. They do not exist in bubbles isolated from each other (but linked through iPhones, flat-screen TVs, and broadband connections like umbilical cords to the powers that be); they participate, voice their opinions and influence each other actively, including through their consumer choices, although not necessarily driven by them.

Two different perspectives on power emerge from the anthology. When analysing specific elite groups or hierarchical relationships (e.g. the nobility in Finland, gender relations, or leadership in companies), those who use power become visible as agents. Thus, the sources of their positions of leverage can be identified and studied. However, in those articles that focus on general historical processes, active participants tend to fade from view and the grammatical passive takes over the narrative; alternatively, power is personified as something larger than the people and their organisations—almost a living creature with a will of its own. Along these lines, Haapala (2010, 32) introduces the 'great octopus' as a metaphor of public power. This type of literary device, while attractive in polemical writing, obscures scholarly research. When power structures are reduced to a metaphorical tentacled monster, familiar from countless political cartoons, or a 'perfect machine that does not seem to work and lacks an operator' (33), the reader is left to fill the gaps with his or her own conspiracy theories. Yet, Haapala maintains that power investigations are an anti-climax for those who expect a spectacular story:

> When it has been stated that power rests with the decision-makers, officials, executives or organisations, the disappointment is obvious because the subconscious expectation seems to be that a conspiracy of the usual suspects ought to be revealed. These can always be found—such as the EU, big business and the IMF—but it is impossible to do anything about them, because they are so far away. Thus, it is easy to oppose them (Haapala, 2010, 33).

Haapala gives no actual example of what he describes, but does not question his own monstrous image of power in anticipation of conspiratorial interpretations. He does not even disprove the conspiracy theory; he merely states that those who wield the greatest power remain out of reach. A citizen's leeway for action seems minuscule. The power investigation does not offer easy answers to this dilemma. In fact, it reveals how much the everyday use of power is an expression of the citizens' acceptance of actual power relations, legitimising the existing order. For example, the article on cartel formation acknowledges that change has already transformed the economic sphere, citing growing globalisation since the 1980s, the great depression of the early 1990s, and the increasing precariousness of the post-depression labour market that affected groups whose access to societal power was already limited (Kallioinen et al., 2010). Even though the Finnish welfare state appears to have remained intact, economic power seems to have increased among the wealthiest. Heiskala and Kantola (2010a) present an even more dismal picture of a deteriorated welfare state in their contribution.

Very few sentences in *Valta Suomessa* addressed issues raised by the recent parliamentary elections in Finland. The appeal of populist parties to voters could be inferred from some lines in the anthology's conclusion (Pietikäinen, 2010b). In a passage on the denial of research supporting the notion of climate change, Pietikäinen suggested that the old adage of the Enlightenment, 'knowledge is power', was distorted to 'influence on opinion is power' (2010b, 255). If media-savvy personalities who spout opinions become politically influential, he asked, where is democracy heading? His straightforward call for increased critical thinking stemmed from the worry that the self-interest of various opinion-makers would blur the common interest. This begs the question of whether lobby groups and vested interests are really something new and unheard of in Finnish policymaking. The programme memorandum posed several crucial questions about the media and their relationship to power elites. The rise of alternative movements, however, was linked to media directed towards a younger audience, assuming that the media took the initiative instead of exploring the possible range of action of new political movements (Akatemia, 2005, 61). A revealing example of some scholars' distance from their research objects and a somewhat narrow definition of the media was Pietikäinen's suggestion that the carnivalesque rock band Lordi did not correspond to 'the mainstream concept of Finnishness' before it became commercialised following its Eurovision Song Contest victory in 2006 (Pietikäinen, 2010a, 17). To anyone in possession of a radio receiver during the last 40 years, this must be an absurd claim.

In the early decades of the twentieth century, Walter Lippmann developed a groundbreaking understanding of the management and manipulation of public opinion. In his view, influence on opinion was power that should be used wisely by cadres of experts (see Lippmann, 1922). The citizens of the Nordic countries do display a high trust in experts, and the legitimation of possibly controversial policies is dependent on expert opinion. However, the question remains: Who watches and controls the experts? In a follow-up newspaper article promoting the VALTA programme, Pietikäinen addressed this problem. He saw the issue of trust and reliability from the citizen's point of view, but after suggesting the impossibility of being thoroughly informed, he placed the responsibility upon the shoulders of the citizen. 'Expert power is functional and controlled when citizens themselves, the very subjects of power, are enlightened and critical,' he maintained. Citizens were expected to become experts with the help of investment in 'a diversified schooling and education' that was meant to enable young people to become watchmen over expert power (Pietikäinen, 2010e, 2). However, it is an open question whether citizens, once they have identified any abuse of expert power, will exercise their own power by informed consumer choices or by appeal to the authorities. As Pietikäinen also states, expertise is used to legitimise decisions made by politicians, whom citizens tend to distrust. It is easy to be critical sitting in front of your own television or posting to an internet forum. The issue is how those in power can truly be held accountable when the citizen's trust has been violated.

An appeal to accountability is made in an article by Heiskala and Kantola on the development of a 'coach state' led by neoliberal principles. According to studies on the hybridisation of public and private power, democracy is endangered by the increasing obscurity of power structures and unclear accountability. If all policy changes are motivated by short-term economic gain, increased competitiveness, and budgetary restraint in public spending, accountability becomes difficult to demand from other perspectives, such as humanitarian and environmental concerns. Heiskala and Kantola (2010a, 133) end their article by claiming that this stereotypical view of people actually corresponded with reality, by contrasting the assumption of increased individualism in current society with the idea of self-determination as a Nordic tradition supported by a free peasantry and Lutheranism. This provides an uncomfortable contrast to Pietikäinen's conclusion that what he sees as typically Finnish submissiveness and respect for authority is deeply rooted in the collective memory (2010b, 256). The Finns are hopefully not doomed to a fate as disinterested consumers in a neoliberal economy without alternatives. If the electorate perceives that votes do not make a difference because all policies are determined by the fixed view that all people are disconnected consumers striving for their own gain, the consequence may be an awakening from complacency.

Such conflicting historical stereotypes about Finnishness are not problematized within VALTA, although scholars are well aware of their origins and political uses in the past. The problematic approach towards individual and collective agency in Finnish scholarly writing has previously been addressed by researchers such as the sociologist Alapuro (2001). Alapuro perceived a lack of analysis of agents and change in Finnish sociology, although studies of social change ought to pay attention to agency. Already in the 1970s, the strong positivist tradition in Finnish sociology, described as 'rooted in logical empiricism', was accused of 'accepting wholesale the existing social system', despite having found space for individual dissenters (Leimu, 1977). Even the alternative Marxist model proposed by the TANDEM report focused on a normative view of agency, prioritising the party as the primary political agent. In the examples from VALTA neither the disconnected individualist idea of the citizen nor the collectivist–corporatist counter-model leave much room for political agency, except among those privileged enough to belong to the elite.

Ylä-Anttila (2010) has summarised the reasons for the pervasiveness of determinist narratives as pressure towards inner unity in the face of external threat and fear of disorder. Although the history of Finland contains many examples of civil disobedience, including civil war, such events do not belong in the grand narrative that emphasises homogeneity and determinism. However, when accountability becomes something that citizens must enforce at the expense of those in power, conflicts are inevitable. In the *Valta Suomessa* articles dealing with this issue, several narratives are gathered that attempt to give meaning to the past, but few of them validate civic agency. Those narratives reveal their hegemonic character by allowing the concept of national homogeneity to override empirical facts. Two alternative national stereotypes were used according to the needs of the writer: the Finnish nation as free and egalitarian, or the Finnish people as submissive to authority. These stereotypes played no analytical role in the articles, except perhaps as openings with which a lay audience might identify. They obscured the opportunity citizens have to organise and struggle for common causes, locally or globally. Similarly, the narrative of an expected increase in individualism clashed with the observed fact of new popular movements and the success of politicians labelled as 'populist'. Such movements may be limited to protest, expressing resistance to 'inevitable' change (the visible ideology of the bourgeois-liberal parties) or the hidden rule of bureaucracy and experts (the policy of necessity); but they are still a powerful force. Increasing demands for accountability may have caused the losses by established political parties in the recent parliamentary elections.

The changes that made the twenty-first-century citizen an allegedly self-interested individualist who merely votes with her or his wallet remained unexplained in light of the studies in the first part of the anthology, which stressed voluntary organisation for collective action among elite groups in the nineteenth-century estate society or in the twentieth-century market economy. Even though the citizen-consumer or prosumer may be politically catchy concepts, it is not self-evident that the citizens of Finland identify themselves with those roles. One critic questioned the usage of catchy slogans like 'coach state' and did not find much evidence for a radical shift away from the nation-state, which remains the main frame of reference for definitions of power relations in Finland (Hannula, 2011). A deeper analysis of the history of a Finnish discourse on power might have provided the programme with a much-needed backbone.

Conclusion

The novel perception of the citizen as a passive consumerist individual, without connections to interest groups or collective efforts, was linked to the hegemonic narrative of the nation's development as a determined process in which conflicts and interest groups are invisible. Even in those cases in which change was identified, the causes or agents behind it remained obscure. No-one can be held accountable if the cause of change is vaguely identified as 'neoliberal principles' without any agent to implement them, or global processes outside of the control of domestic actors. While certainly not all of the projects in the VALTA programme have promoted this view, the programme results have been packaged in such a narrative. In the cases in which the results of individual projects have been embedded in different narratives, their connection to the VALTA programme has been obscured. This fragmentation might have been a consequence of the Academy's conscious goal of producing politically independent research in stark contrast to the Scandinavian power investigations. While that goal was reached, the reluctance to draw overall political conclusions on the basis of the projects is reflected in the cautious, passive wording of the articles written by the programme coordinator. The resulting dissatisfaction expressed in the evaluation report might have been averted by a more conflict-oriented presentation of the results, but this was not necessarily the intention or in the best interest of the researchers.

If the programme's intention was to reach a scholarly audience, as Norbert Götz suggests in this volume, it did not succeed: the programme attracted nowhere near the attention that TANDEM had aroused. Individual projects generated debate and further research, but they maintained their independent character and rather loose ties to the programme. The 2012 evaluation report described the media strategy of the VALTA programme in dismissive terms, with the mollifying observation that the programme coordinator did make an effort to reach out to stakeholders, although the projects themselves prioritised completing their own research plans. The evaluators consequently recommended that the Academy of Finland promote a 'more proactive, more interactive and more internationally oriented' programme outreach (Evaluation panel, 2012, 22). TANDEM may have set a precedent with its outspoken goal of giving a unified presentation of a Finnish system of governance and its economic foundations. The text of the 2012 evaluation report implies that something similar was expected of VALTA, despite its clearly different umbrella character and the open, pluralistic, interdisciplinary goals set in the 2005 programme memorandum.

A power investigation that does not make any attempt to shake the foundations of power may, nevertheless, be influential. In Norway, the *Makt- og demokratiutredningen* (Public Investigation on Power and Democracy) generated public interest and a lively debate, although its goals corresponded with the traditional functions of public investigations on power: to provide a long-term policy for social and legal change and to mediate between different organisations and parties by providing arguments based on the work of the expert committee.

The lack of public attention and media interest in VALTA was certainly not intended. It may have been the programme's underestimation of civic power that has kept public interest in it low. The Academy of Finland's objective of maintaining its independence from political influence did distinguish the VALTA programme from its Scandinavian predecessors, but distanced it from the public discourse on policy-making and agenda setting.

Notes

[1] See Suomen Akatemia (2005; available online in Finnish, Swedish, and English, at: http://www.aka.fi/Tiedostot/Tiedostot/VALTA/Ohjelmamuistio%20(pdf).pdf), Pietikäinen (2010c; available online, in Finnish, at: http://www.aka.fi/Tiedostot/Tiedostot/VALTA/VALTA%20Hankkeiden%20tulokset.pdf), Pietikäinen (2010d; available in Finnish at: http://www.aka.fi/Tiedostot/Tiedostot/VALTA/VALTA%20E-lehteen.pdf), and Evaluation panel (2012; available in English online at: http://www.aka.fi/Tiedostot/Tiedostot/Julkaisut/2_12_VALTA.pdf).

[2] VALTA seminar 23 April 2012, speeches by Professor Marja Järvelä (Chair of the evaluation panel), Professor Raimo Väyrynen, Director General Juhana Vartiainen (Government Institute for Economic Research), Professor Teivo Teivainen, Professor Marja Keränen et al.

[3] What Pietikäinen meant with the latter term remained unexplained, but it may be assumed that he referred to theories of rational choice.

References

Alapuro, R. 2001. "Missä ovat toimijat?" *Sosiologia* 1: 51–57.

Anonymous, 2013, "Professori: Suomessa politiikot voivat kulkea töppäyksestä toiseen." Taloussanomat, 21 March 2013. Accessed June 10, 2013. http://www.taloussanomat.fi/politiikka/2013/03/21/professori-suomessa-politiikot-voivat-kulkea-toppayksesta-toiseen/20134327/12

Bengtsson, Å., and M. Mattila. 2011. "Finlandssvenskarnas demokrativisioner: Mer medborgarinflytande eller skuggdemokrati?" In *Språk och politisk mobilisering – Finlandssvenskar i publikdemokrati*, edited by K. Grönlund, 111–134. Helsingfors: SLS.

Edenheim, S. 2010. "Politics Out of Time – Historical Expertise and Temporal Claims in Swedish Governmental Reports." In *In Experts We Trust – Knowledge, Politics and Bureaucracy in Nordic Welfare States*, edited by Å. Lundqvist, and K. Petersen, 35–58. Odense: University Press of Southern Denmark.

Evaluation panel. 2012. *Research Programme on Power and Society in Finland (VALTA) 2007–2010 – Evaluation Report*. Publications of the Academy of Finland 2/12. Helsinki: Academy of Finland.

Gronow, J., P. Klemola, and J. Partanen. 1977. *Demokratian rajat ja rakenteet. Tutkimus suomalaisesta hallitsemistavasta ja sen taloudellisesta perustasta*. Juva: WSOY.

Haapala, P. 2010. "Vallan rakenteet ja yhteiskunnan muutos: Mielikuvaharjoitus 1800–2000-lukujen Suomesta." In *Valta Suomessa*, edited by P. Pietikäinen, 21–33. Helsinki: Gaudeamus.

Hämäläinen, U. 2010. "Suomi takaisin Sorsan aikaan." *Helsingin Sanomat*, 11 June 2010, C, p. 1.

Hannula, M. 2011. "Ota kiinni mistä saat." *niin & näin* 4/11, Accessed June 10, 2013. http://netn.fi/lehti/niin-nain-411/ota-kiinni-mist%C3%A4-saat

Heiskala, R., and A. Kantola. 2010a. "Vallan uudet ideat: hyvinvointivaltion huomasta valmentajavaltion valvontaan." In *Valta Suomessa*, edited by P. Pietikäinen, 124–148. Helsinki: Gaudeamus.

Heiskala, R., and A. Kantola. 2010b. "Emme kaipaa 1970-luvulle." *Helsingin Sanomat*, 12 June 2010, C, p. 5.

Helkama, K., R. Paloniemi, T. Rantala, A. Vainio, and A. Valkeapää. 2010. "Kiistakapulana metsät: Suomen metsä- ja luonnonsuojelupolitiikan hyväksyttävyys." In *Valta Suomessa*, edited by P. Pietikäinen, 149–168. Helsinki: Gaudeamus.

Jääsaari, J., U. Kivikuru, M. Aslama, and J. Juntunen. 2010. "Median tuottama kansalaisuus: Tulkintaa raameista ja rakenteista." In *Valta Suomessa*, edited by P. Pietikäinen, 210–228. Helsinki: Gaudeamus.

Kalela, J. 2008. "Perinteisen politiikan loppu." In *Suomalaisen yhteiskunnan poliittinen historia*, edited by V. Pernaa, and M. K. Niemi, 244–264. Helsinki: Edita, Kleio.

Kallioinen, M., J. Keskinen, L. Lähteenmäki, T. Paavonen, and K. Teräs. 2010. "Kilpailun voittokulku: Kartelleista ja säännöstelystä globaaliin markkinatalouteen." In *Valta Suomessa*, edited by P. Pietikäinen, 56–78. Helsinki: Gaudeamus.

Kivistö, P., and P. Kraus, eds. forthcoming. *Challenging Power: Equality, Culture and Minorities*. New York: Palgrave Macmillan.

Koivunen, A., and M. Lehtonen. 2011. *Kuinka meitä kutsutaan? Kulttuuriset merkityskamppailut nyky-Suomessa*. Helsinki: Vastapaino.

Kortteinen, M. 2008. "Elämmekö laantuvien ristiriitojen ja hyvän hallinnan aikaa?" In *Tarkemmin ajatellen – Kansakunnan henkinen tila*, edited by I. Niiniluoto, and J. Sihvola, 195–220. Helsinki: Gaudeamus.

Lapintie, K. 2010. "Voittaako valta järjen? Tieto ja valta kaupunkikehityksessä." In *Valta Suomessa*, edited by P. Pietikäinen, 99–123. Helsinki: Gaudeamus.

Lehtonen, M., and A. Koivunen. 2010. "Median ihannesubjektit ja suostumuksen tuottaminen." In *Valta Suomessa*, edited by P. Pietikäinen, 229–250. Helsinki: Gaudeamus.

Leimu, H. 1977. "Sociology in Finland. Notes on Main Traditions in Sociology and on Some of their Exponents with an Emphasis on the Period Since 1945." *Zeitschrift für Soziologie* 6 (2): 222–249.

Lippmann, W. 1922. *Public Opinion*. New York: Harcourt, Brace and Company.

Loima, J. 2006. *Myytit, uskomukset ja kansa – Johdanto moderniin nationalismiin Suomessa 1809 – 1918*. Helsinki: Yliopistopaino.

Mäkinen, I. 2002. "Radikalismin vuosikymmenet (1960–1980-luvut) Suomen kirjastomaailmassa." *Informaatiotutkimus* 21 (1): 10–23.

Ojala, S. 2010. "Yhteiskuntatieteilijöiden näkökulmia kaivataan keskusteluun hyvinvoinnista." *Helsingin Sanomat*, 17 June 2010, C, p. 6.

Partanen, J. 1992. "1970-luku: TANDEM." *Sosiologia* 3: 193–199.

Pietikäinen, P. 2010a. "Johdanto: Epäilyttävä, houkutteleva valta." In *Valta Suomessa*, edited by P. Pietikäinen, 7–18. Helsinki: Gaudeamus.

Pietikäinen, P. 2010b. "Lopuksi: Kansalaiset valtaa vahtimassa." In *Valta Suomessa*, edited by P. Pietikäinen, 251–259. Helsinki: Gaudeamus.

Pietikäinen, P. 2010c. *Valta-ohjelman hankkeiden tulokset*. Helsinki: Suomen Akatemia.

Pietikäinen, P. 2010d. *VALTA-ohjelma loppui mutta vallan tutkimus jatkuu*. Helsinki: Suomen Akatemia.

Pietikäinen, P. 2010e. "Asiantuntijavaltakin tarvitsee vahtikoiransa." *Helsingin Sanomat*, 2 December 2010, A, p. 2.

Rautkallio, H., and M. Häikiö. 1977. *Demokratia ja tasa-arvo – Arvioita painopistetutkimuksista TANDEM ja DETA*, 79–114. Helsinki: WSOY.

Ruostetsaari, I. 2010. "Energiapolitiikan hallinta: Kuluttajakansalainen ja edustuksellisen demokratian oikeutus." In *Valta Suomessa*, edited by P. Pietikäinen, 169–190. Helsinki: Gaudeamus.

Ruuskanen, O. -P., A. Snellman, and M. Widgrén. 2010. "Yhteiskunnan huipulla: Eliittirakenne muutoksessa 1809–2009." In *Valta Suomessa*, edited by P. Pietikäinen, 34–55. Helsinki: Gaudeamus.

Saari, J. 2010. "Valtaa etsimässä." *Yhteiskuntapolitiikka* 75 (5): 572–573.

Sulkunen, P. 1977. "TANDEM demokratiasta." *Tiede ja edistys* 3: 64–68.

Sulkunen, P. 2010. "TANDEM-trauma." *Sosiologia* 3: 235–237.

Suomen Akatemia. 2005. *Valta Suomessa (VALTA) 2007–2010-tutkimusohjelma. Ohjelmamuistio (Programme memorandum)*. Helsinki: Suomen Akatemia.

Toiviainen, S. 1977. "KTTS tiedepoliisina." *Tiede ja edistys* 1: 1–7.

Vesikansa, J. 1976. *Esimerkki tutkimuksen harharetkistä. Arvioita Tandemin osatutkimuksesta Mainonta ja yhteiskunta*. Helsinki: KTTS:n julkaisusarja 18.

Ylä-Anttila, T. 2010. *Politiikan paluu – Globalisaatioliike ja julkisuus*. Tampere: Vastapaino.

Justice and EU Foreign Policy

ALEX PRICHARD

University of Exeter, UK

ABSTRACT   *In this article I argue that the contemporary normative analysis of EU foreign policy is predominantly Kantian. This, I argue, is highly problematic, because at the heart of Kantian and neo-Kanitan accounts of ethics is a moral universalism that ought not to animate EU foreign policy unless that foreign policy desires to be neo-colonial. I set out why this is the case by developing an account of ethics derived from the writings of Alasdair MacIntyre. MacIntyre's account of ethics is both critical of Kantian universalism and provides a constructive alternative for evaluating moral behaviour and I use both sets of insights to evaluate neo-Kantianism in EU studies and liberal universalism as a suitable foundation for an ethical foreign policy of the EU.*

Introduction

Over the past 10 years, debates in EU studies surrounding how or why we might consider the EU to be an ethical or normative power have proliferated (Manners 2002; Whitman 2011b). This paper looks less at the issues that might sustain an empirical claim regarding the EU's moral character, and more at the 'how' or meta-ethical questions, that is, how and on which ethical grounds should we evaluate whether the EU is being moral when it acts beyond its borders? At the heart of this question is a prior and necessary debate about how we understand the meaning and content of justice. Where does justice come from? How would we know if it had been attained? My claim in this paper is that answers to these questions in relation to the EU have typically been framed in Kantian terms and that this is hugely problematic if we desire to move beyond the 'essentialism' and 'neo-colonialism' associated with conceptions of 'ethical foreign policy' and 'civilian power Europe', respectively (Whitman 2011, 4).

    While the debates in this area have become hugely complicated and extensive, let me be clear from the outset that this paper engages only with the complications that arise with Kantian framings of the ethics of EU foreign policy. This is primarily a meta-ethical and meta-theoretical paper. I do not claim to be an expert in the nitty-gritty of EU foreign relations or in the extensive debates that have emerged in this area. My principal claim is to have spotted an important confusion which I wish to clarify and correct. Having set out the parameters of this confusion, I argue against Kantian approaches to foreign policy in

EU studies and for virtue ethics as a more appropriate set of ethical tools for evaluating EU foreign policy.

The prevalence of Kantianism in debates around the ethics of EU foreign policy mirrors the prevalence of Kantianism across the wider IR literature. Since the 1970s and the re-emergence of normative or explicitly moral-philosophical approaches to international relations, neo-Kantianism has arguably reigned supreme (see, e.g., Doyle 1983; Hurrel 1990; Nardin 2006; Walzer 1992). The hallmark of neo-Kantian positions in IR has been the equation of justice and morality with mutually agreed-upon rules that can bind behaviour and the ethical principles that ought to underpin those rules, which by their moral force we ought to be compelled to follow. Justice, it is claimed, is only possible in a politico-legal system in which the freedom of one is the precondition of the freedom of all (Rosen 1993, 6–39) and central to realising this ideal, then, is a system of laws and rules that sets the parameters for freedom. These rules can, it is argued, be deduced rationally either from *a priori* first principles or maxims, such as 'impartiality' or 'do least harm' (Barry 1995; Linklater 2012), or from something that is essential to humans *qua* humans, such as moral learning and communication (Habermas 1990), or from the structure of rationality itself (Kant 1964; Rawls 1971). But across this approach it is the rules that constitute our freedom, and so the purpose of moral philosophy is to provide the foundations for such a claim.[1]

That Kant and later Kantians found the immanent fulfilment of reason and morality in liberal (sometimes social) democratic republicanism is well known. Kagan's (2002) ironic jibe that the EU is a Kantian 'paradise' reflects the widely perceived, if largely unarticulated view that Europe has come closest to the final stage in this providentialist narrative. For many, the universalist aspirations of the EU's founding principles are what typify this moral force. The assumption seems to be that, as the EU grows, develops and extends beyond its borders, it would then almost automatically have right on its side, simply by virtue of *what it is* (Manners 2002).

This paper takes issue with this way of understanding ethics and the EU. The reasons for this are political, analytical and normative. We must ask ourselves, is it adequate to conceptualise EU moral agency in Kantian terms when it comes to exercising the use of force beyond its borders or when it seeks to mediate between conflict parties? To assume that by virtue of having devised the norms that the enforcement and extension of them is unproblematic, is to reify both the EU and to ignore the very neo-colonialism at the heart of the globalisation of the liberal and neo-liberal project. While I do not wish to argue the merits or otherwise of human rights or liberal democratic norms here, what concerns me more is the automatic equation of both with justice and their universalisation with right moral action. On what grounds is it right to assume that such a project is good? This is the question that concerns me here.

What if, as MacIntyre (1988) suggested, the very foundations of this neo-Kantian vision are flawed? What if reason or our moral sense are without foundations, our framing of them empirically inaccurate and ultimately undermining of the very project it seeks to realise? What if rule-following is not an adequate foundation for right but rather the tacit acceptance of the status quo, or worse? What if there are alternative ways of understanding the basis of justice, ways that are non-deterministic, sociological and historical? What would this reframing do to our understanding of justice and the EU as an actor and how might we use this reframing of the concept of justice to articulate a new understanding of the ethics of EU foreign policy?

To this end, this paper seeks to contribute to the debates surrounding 'the ethical dilemmas' generated by, and the 'justifications behind, the exercise of [EU] power' beyond its borders (Aggestam 2008, 3). In order to do so, I take a neo-Aristotelian approach to this subject, informed by the work of Alasdair Macintyre, the key late-twentieth-century reference for the re-articulation of Aristotelian 'virtue ethics'. The paper has both a critical and a constructive part. The critical argument is that neo-Kantian approaches to the ethics of EU foreign policy exclude the social and historical determinants of right in favour of positing rational maxims which are purported to have universal validity. As Kant put it, the maxims that underpin the categorical imperative are *a priori* or, literally, *beyond experience*. This approach to the morality of foreign policy is problematic since, as I show, it leads to the equation of justice to the following of rules and a tendency to see the existing legal architecture as the benchmark of justice. It also elides the socio-historical complexity of world politics.

Virtue ethics, while a plural field of research in its own right (Crisp 1996), asks us to approach claims to justice and right sociologically and historically. That is to say, that claims and competing claims to justice and right must be understood in context as it is this context that gives meaning to right. For example, for virtue ethicists, what it means to be a good father is dependent, to an important degree, on the context within which fathering is to be realised, the practices within which fatherhood is ensconced and the institutions available to defend and sustain those practices. Can we expect the same of a starving father and his family in the Democratic Republic of Congo as we might of his more affluent middle-class counterpart in Norway? If the answer is no, then universalism as a basis for ethics is null and void.

The paper proceeds in the following way. After a critical discussion of Kantian approaches to ethics and foreign policy, I set out in broad terms an alternative way of understanding foreign policy and international relations based on a MacIntyrean understanding of virtue ethics. I focus on three main insights. First, I unpack in broad terms the neo-Aristotelian critique of rule-based conceptions of morality, specifically the critique of rationalism; second, I show the context-oriented method that virtue ethicists pursue and outline the varieties of context and their causal powers in relation to morality and justice; finally, I set out how these understandings of virtue might translate into empirical studies of foreign policy.

In the second, more substantial part of the paper, I apply this theoretical discussion to the study of the ethics of EU foreign policy. I begin by providing an all-too-potted analysis of conceptions of justice articulated in the official policy documents of the EU. My aim here is to illustrate the minimalist, formalistic, positive conceptions of justice that are articulated by the EU, conceptions that suggest that for all intents and purposes justice *is* the rule of law for the EU. I then turn to the growing academic literature within EU studies that has sought to provide grounds for evaluating the EU's foreign policy behaviour on moral grounds. What I show is that here, too, the tendency is towards neo-Kantianism. Here, the academic literature also assumes that the existing laws and universal principles proclaimed by the EU are, *a priori*, the basis for justice, equating the status quo with a transcendent conception of right.

What I show is that in some cases the neo-imperialism/neo-colonialism of this position is clear, and many empirical evaluations of the EU's normative credentials indicate just this (see, e.g., Chandler 2004, 2006; Diez and Pace 2011; Juncos 2011). Forcing others to abide by laws they have had no hand in writing is hardly a solid foundation for right, and presuming the EU to have right on its side by virtue of what *it is* is no less hubristic. If, as Whitman, Manners and others argue, Europe and the scholars who have been assessing its ethical credentials are to avoid charges of neo-colonialism and essentialism, more explicit reflection on this basic problem is needed.

Kantian Ethics and EU Foreign Policy

The Kantian tradition is perhaps the most prolific in twentieth-century ethics, and it would be futile to try and summarise it here. Instead, my aim is to set out the meta-ethics of the tradition's key theorist: Immanuel Kant. By meta-ethics, I mean the underlying theory of Kant's theory of justice. Rather than focus on the principles of distributive justice or cosmopolitanism, what I want to answer is the following: Where does Kantian justice come from, or on what grounds is something just in the Kantian schema? This brief foray is central to our comprehension of the muddle surrounding contemporary thinking about ethics in relation to EU foreign policy, particularly in relation to the concept of Europe as a normative power. But it is also central to understanding precisely what virtue ethics can bring to this debate.

For Kant, justice and law are interlinked. The law is right when it is the expression of justice, and justice must be the expression of universal or transcendental maxims such as the famous 'categorical imperative'. But where does the imperative to live life according to universalisable maxims come from? Kant argues that we can deduce the rational architecture of right from the structures of reason itself. Since the faculty of reason is universal (though we are differentially endowed with it), ideas can potentially be shared by all rational humans. Through rational reflection we can all, at least potentially, gain access to the universal principles of justice that can bring political harmony to the world we live in. The onus is on the legislators, since it is they who must set down the rules for those who cannot reason sufficiently well (barbarians, women, children, etc). Plumbing the depths of reason

> 'will enable him [the jurist] to lay the foundations of all possible positive legislations. And while empirical laws may give him valuable guidance, a purely empirical theory of right ... may have a fine appearance, but will unfortunately contain no brain.' (Kant 1991a, 132)

By this, Kant means that circumstance and context are too fluid and varied. To leave law to respond to this would thus denude it of what gives it human character – reason. Since reason is potentially universal, this is the only true basis for right. By this framing, morality is deontological, which is to say it is beyond the phenomenal realm 'out there' and is transcendent. Transcendence implies that the principles derived from the structures of pure reason have a universal quality untouched by time and place, because they are common to all men in all places and because we share the possibility of critical reason, even if our abilities are not equally shared (Kant 1993). To let the real, phenomenal world in would not only undermine our ability to reason autonomously; it would also suggest that factors other than reason can shape our conceptions of right and wrong, that we might be pushed and pulled by circumstance and that as individuals we are therefore not always wholly responsible for our actions. For Kant, the universal moral law is as constant as

Newton's physical law, but the two domains are ontologically distinct. In the *Groundwork*, Kant put it like this:

> pure philosophy (that is, metaphysics) must come first, and without it there can be no moral philosophy at all. Indeed a philosophy which mixes up these pure principles with empirical ones does not deserve the name of philosophy (since philosophy is distinguished from ordinary rational knowledge precisely because it sets forth in a separate science what the latter apprehends only as confused with other things). Still less does it deserve the name of moral philosophy since by this very confusion it undermines even the purity of morals themselves and acts against its own proper purpose. (Kant 1964, 58)

From these assumptions Kant develops his famous categorical imperative. It was stated thus: 'Act only on that maxim through which you can at the same time will that it should become a universal law' (Kant 1964, 88). In matters of right, law and justice, the categorical imperative translates as: 'Every action which by itself or by its maxim enables the freedom of each individual's will to co-exist with the freedom of everyone else in accordance with a universal law is *right*' (Kant 1991a, 133). Thus, justice must first be deduced from the universal maxims of morality, which are themselves given in the structure of reason itself, and from this one must deduce the corresponding laws. In this way, justice becomes synonymous with a deontological or maxim-informed set of laws.

It is not difficult to see how we move from rule-based maxims of ethics to the moral underpinnings of laws, but the issue for Kant is far more expansive than this. If laws are rational, the legal and political system becomes the precondition for bringing human activity into transcendent harmony with itself and the rational laws that govern the universe. So, states become enlightened in so far as they cohere with the principles of political right, and international order can only be guaranteed if the republican constitution is spread worldwide, thereby assuring that freedoms secured in one state are not undermined by the pursuit of irrational barbarism by those beyond the federation (Kant 1991c; cf. Behnke 2008).

Kant's republican advance on the absolutism of the Old Regime was to replace the identification of the state with an individual, with the identification of the moral state with a set of republican laws (Tuck 2001). These laws needed the willing agreement and minimal participation of republican political subjects for their moral force, but, nonetheless, the state becomes the aggregate of the plural autonomous sovereign individuals. Both individuals and states became bearers of *moral* agency by virtue of the establishment of republican constitutions. The immediate Hobbesian problem that emerged, of how to ensure that the first-order anarchy between individuals in a state of nature was not replicated at the international level between states, was one Kant grappled with throughout his final years. In the 'Idea of a Universal History' (1991b) and 'Perpetual Peace' (1999c), he argues that, unfortunately, war will inevitably be the way through which liberal principles are exported to those not yet privy to enlightenment and that through this process of slow expansion of republican constitutionalism throughout the international realm, international relations will be pacified in a manner that mirrored processes underway at the domestic level.

From this perspective, liberal imperialism was at the heart of the liberal republican project (for more on this, see Jahn 2000, 2005, 2009). For Fukuyama (1989), 'the end of history' was symbolised by the 'common marketization' of the world in the EEC's image. The question we need to ask is whether the ethical framing that underpins this liberal ideology is appropriate for an institution such as the EU, given the legacy of imperialism it is trying to overcome? If the EU wishes to be context-specific in its dealings with third-party states, can or should the EU assume that it has right is on its side or that it is moral by virtue of *what it is*, simply because quasi and neo-Kantian norms of juridical rectitude are ascribed to it by academics and simply by virtue of the fact that is a nominally republican union?

Virtue Ethics and International Relations

One way of illustrating the problems with this framing of ethics is to turn to virtue ethics. The existing literature on virtue ethics and IR is minimal (Brown 2010; Gaskarth 2011, 2012; Mani 2002; Tsakatika 2008), but the concerns with rule following as a basis for ethics are shared. Typically, these writers argue, ethical thinking in IR has been framed around questions of the moral efficacy of state borders, that moral thinking in mainstream thinking derives responsibility from law and reason and suggests right moral action is action that is rule-following. There is a general discontent amongst virtue ethicists that context is downplayed in mainstream thinking about ethics and the creeping universalism of moral reason elides the agonistic social basis for morality. While it is impossible to do justice to the sophistication of this literature here, a few words should help show its pertinence in this general context before I briefly develop the meta-ethics of this position in the following section.

For example, Chris Brown has argued that the cosmopolitan/communitarian debate is both flawed and unhelpful from the perspective of virtue ethics. Brown argued that both cosmopolitans and communitarians presupposed a quasi-liberal and Kantian vision of the individual, an individual who was able to choose rationally between two *a priori* sets of ethical priorities. The question asked is: Should I identify with my community or a global community of rational, rights-bearing individuals? But from the perspective of virtue ethics it is impossible to think about communal or universal moral communities without doing so from the perspective of a community-bound or sociologically specific individual. Some people may wish to identify with a cosmopolis, others not. In short, the communitarian/cosmopolitan debate presents us with a false dichotomy that only makes sense within a generally Kantian framing, one that assumes a universal political subject capable of deciding and labouring under the presupposition that their decision would have universal reach.

At the turn of the millennium, the tendency within debates surrounding transitional justice was to equate the establishment of the rule of law with the realisation of justice itself. Mani (2002, 2005a, 2005b) asked the following question: If law, including the institutions through which it is delivered and enforced, is the very embodiment of justice, is establishing the rule of law all that is needed to achieve justice in post-conflict societies? Echoing advocates of the liberal peace (see, e.g., Doyle 1983, 1986) many suggested that a Kantian peace required republican and liberal democratic institutions and slowly but surely, the ideological content of the liberal world-view was lost as the seemingly irrefutable empirical realities led to moralising US hegemony. In practice, however, Mani argued that a 'minimalist position' was adopted by peace-building agencies. Rather than explicitly endorse the moral credentials of the credentials of the liberal rule of law, law and justice were terms that were used interchangeably and seen to be largely coterminous – indeed, in many cases they still are in popular discourse in the West too (Mani 2002, 26– 30). However, this framing provides no analytical or critical purchase on questions of social justice. The equation of law with justice means that issues of distributive and social justice were redressed through the courts in post-conflict contexts. This undermined the social practices needed to sustain recovery in the long term by arrogating to the courts (usually imposed by the West from the outside) the right to decide and to legislate, with now well-known consequences (see, e.g., Sriram 2007; Paris 2004; Richmond 2006).

Tsakatika (2008) has deployed virtue ethics approaches to explain the corruption scandal that rocked and eventually forced the resignation of the Santer Commission in 1999. Following rules in this case was clearly inadequate since the rules and laws were set down by those who circumnavigated them. Rather than establish ever more rules, Tsakatika suggests that a more fruitful place to start might be to foster those virtues of responsibility and accountability, which were lacking in this instance, amongst EU technocrats. This 'internal' analysis of the EU from a virtue ethics perspective is crying out for an 'external' companion piece.

There is some precedent here for the study of foreign policy from a virtue ethics perspective, but it is a little individualist in focus. Gaskarth (2011) has sought to revive thinking about virtues in order to provide a system of ethical critique that focuses on the character of individual foreign policymakers. His turn to character allows him to avoid the tendency to evaluate the decisions of foreign policymakers according to rules, which themselves need ethical justification (and so on in infinite regress) and rarely seem to constrain agency or dissuade actors from providing non-legal virtue-based justifications for their actions – Tony Blair being the focal point of Gaskarth's piece. Gaskarth argues that Foreign Policy Analysis (FPA) might be profitably developed by setting out the appropriate character traits that decision-makers ought to cultivate if they are to be able to exercise good moral judgement in specific international contexts; for it seems that this, rather than rules, seems to be the criterion by which people usually justify and evaluate actions.

What I want to do next is develop these openings in order to flesh out how the work of MacIntyre can help us approach EU foreign policy. To this end, three inter-related concepts are central: virtues, practices and institutions. Practices are,

> any coherent and complex form of socially embedded established cooperative human activity through which goods internal to that form of activity are realised in the course of trying to achieve those standards of excellence which are appropriate to, and partially definitive of, that form of activity, with the result that human powers to achieve excellence, and human conceptions of the ends and goods involved, are systematically extended. (MacIntyre 1981, 175)

Practices can involve building cities, playing chess or football, or writing an academic paper. Within these practices, the virtues indicate socially agreed standards of excellence towards which those who aspire to excellence will gear their activities. MacIntyre defines the virtues as 'an acquired human quality the possession and exercise of which tends to enable us to achieve those goods which are internal to practices and the lack of which effectively prevents us from achieving any such goods' (1981, 178).

For MacIntyre, society is structured through practices and morality is central to shaping the way we act within those practices. Indeed, what is moral does not travel well outside those practices. This is not to claim that virtue ethicists are communitarians, valorising a community over a cosmopolis, just that when we compare and debate the virtues, we must be sensitive to the contexts within which practices are ensconced. The virtues are moral in the sense that they lead us to aspire to 'the good' (as opposed to material goods) and provide reasons for avoiding vices, not because they chime with the subterranean beat of human consciousness evolving to an ever-higher rationality in some dim and distant future. Vices, on the other hand, will be those conscious activities, like plagiarism, that systematically undermine the *practices* within which the virtues, like scholarly integrity, are given meaning and are realised. Both practices and virtues are therefore co-dependent. From this perspective, MacIntyre argues that 'it is not clear to me ... how *any* adequate philosophical analysis in this area [of morality] could escape being also a sociological hypothesis, and *vice versa*' (MacIntyre 1981, 70).

MacIntyre develops a Marxist-inspired understanding of the role of class in shaping the social and political context within which certain virtues are promoted and defended (for more, see Blackledge and Davidson 2008; Horton and Mendus 1994). What does this involve? If I desire such and such, working to attain that desired object will constitute the *telos* of my actions. My means and the values I embody in pursuing that end are integral to and prefigure the ends themselves. Since we are all constrained by our class position (not to mention race, gender and geographic location) to some degree, the goods we defend and aspire to are inevitably socially structured, as are our conceptions of them. There are no transcendent goods or values and none can be universalised. So, MacIntyre sees our moral *telos* to be relatively structured within the practices and institutions we inhabit. This leaves open the question of progress, of the nature of rationality and of the sorts of institutions we might wish to build and does not deny that we inevitably have competing visions of the good. Finally, virtue ethics does not valorise the law and suggests we see the law as much as the expression of power as of the expression of right (cf. Anghie 2005).

MacIntyre's views on institutions would also council against reifying or moralising them. While he argues that practices and virtues without institutions to defend them would be fatally vulnerable, there is no natural synergy between an institution or set of institutions and the virtues and practices a population holds dear. Institutions, from football clubs to the EU, are 'characteristically and necessarily concerned with ... external goods. They are involved in acquiring money and other material goods; they are structured in terms of power and status, and they distribute money, power and status as rewards'. They do this to sustain themselves and 'the practices of which they are the bearers' (MacIntyre 1981, 181). Unlike the ideology of the moral state we find in Kantian and liberal ideology, for MacIntyre there is no necessary synergy between virtues and institutions or between individuals and institutions. Simply put, institutions are not agents, but structures within which agents act (Wight 2006). Institutions constrain and enable individual and group agency in differential ways depending on the subject position of the individual group within that institution and the positioning of groups and individuals relative to one another (Are groups and individuals dominated, enabled by others? Do they occupy privileged positions? Are they materially better off?).

Part of the problem with contemporary accounts of the EU's moral agency is precisely this – it is considered to have one. This is a simple act of reification, even fetishism. As I argued above, it was the nineteenth-century liberal republicans who did most to cast the state as a moral person, the equivalent of the rational universal moral political subject that was necessary to undergird the law. This monistic ideology of political agency infuses our political ontology today such that it makes evaluating the EU's behaviour very difficult indeed. As the multi-level governance literature (Marks, Hooghe, and Blank 1996) indicates, not to mention the declaiming voices that surrounded the EU's lack of coherence and effectiveness in Bosnia over the last two decades (Juncos, 2013), the EU is at best a constellation of institutions that rarely if ever allow individuals and groups to pull in the same way. A far more fruitful focus for moral judgement is individuals, groups and the institutional context within which they operate. This reframing demands that we avoid the reification of the EU and refuse the simple and deceptive equation of EU agency with moral agency.

Conceptions of Justice in the Formal EU Documentation

So, how do the formal EU documents frame questions of justice? 'The EU Charter of Fundamental Rights' makes reference to any number of virtues that contemporary Europeans hold dear, from 'human dignity, freedom, equality and solidarity' (Preamble) to 'non-discrimination' (Article 21), to an entire section devoted to 'Solidarity' (Title IV). However, when it comes to 'Justice' (Title VI) the EU Charter of Fundamental Rights is quite clear that what is meant is simply the rule of law and due process (European Commission 2010), a paradigm case of 'minimalism' in the sense outlined by Rama Mani (above). The European Commission document 'Underwriting Justice for All' (European Commission 2009) states that its aim is to ensure that justice is 'accessible to all'. 'EU support in this area deals with judiciary, courts and prisons.' Also, 'transitional justice' refers to 'post-conflict situations [wherein] justice is often part of security sector reform approach.' When we look at what it means for the EU to be an 'Area of Freedom, Security and Justice', what the relevant EU documents refer to is upholding the rule of law under the first and third pillar of the community. When we turn to the Lisbon Treaty, we see that justice is also predominantly defined in this juridical sense, referring either to the Court of Justice, and 'access to justice' or the 'Area of Freedom Security and Justice'. In the European Commission's publicity document *Freedom, Security and Justice for All: Justice and Home Affairs in the European Union,* justice is either undefined or conflated with 'development of effective justice systems across the world' (European Commission 2004, 4). Legal justice, criminal justice and justice systems are more or less the limit of formal EU conceptions of right.

Sometimes, however, the EU documents hint at wider conceptions of justice. For example, Article 3 of the Treaty of the EU refers in passing to 'social justice': 'The Union shall combat social exclusion and discrimination, and shall promote social justice and protection, equality between women and men, solidarity between generations and protection of the rights of the child.' Elsewhere, the European Security Strategy states that '[f]lows of trade and investment, the development of technology and the spread of democracy have brought freedom and prosperity to many people. Others have perceived globalisation as a cause of frustration and *injustice*' (European Council 2003: Section 1, emphasis added). In neither instance is the concept of justice defined precisely, and the problem that attends to this is clear. Can global trade regulations be both legal and unjust at once? Is the pursuit of social justice compatible with the existing legal architecture of the global order? How could we know if the laws are unjust and what are the problems we face in attempting to craft a vocabulary of injustice and a practice of justice-seeking if the very things we are asked to see as the manifestation of justice are those things that patently are not so. However, such a lexicon and normative framework cannot be found within EU documents, in which 'minimalist' accounts of justice predominate.

Turning to the EU's emerging practices of 'transitional justice', Crossley-Frolick (2009) has unpicked the EU's implicit and emerging strategy from the tangled web of policy instruments and institutions being developed at present. Of particular interest are the EU's moves towards prosecuting human rights violations, democracy promotion, promoting the rule of law and development, all through the Commission and its right of initiative. The defence of these practices is based on global legal convention. This is not in and of itself unethical or immoral, but it does suggest that the EU has conflated what is right with what is legal. Elsewhere, the European Security Strategy makes clear that,

> The quality of international society depends on the quality of the governments that are its foundation. The best protection for our security is a world of well-governed democratic states. Spreading good governance, supporting social and political reform, dealing with corruption and abuse of power, establishing the rule of law and protecting human rights are the best means of strengthening the international order. (European Council 2003, 10)

This position is defended by most liberal states and is usually accompanied by market reforms and privatisation. However, there is little reflection in the policy documents as to why this model of justice is preferred over any other. Are we to concede the neo-liberal argument that a nominal liberal peace provides a template to end history?

If we turn to the academic literature, it tends not to depart substantively from this general neo-Kantian framing. Ian Manners described justice as 'a particular/culture transcending norm' (2006, 170). Elsewhere, Scheipers and Sicurelli have argued that 'European elites and officials represent the EU as strongly committed to international law and therefore as a major sponsor of justice and order in international relations' (2007, 453). Federica Bicci argues that 'the normative core' of such values as 'social justice', as referred to in various sections of the Treaty of Europe, are 'defined on the basis of the universality of values' embedded in international law and the various UN declarations (2006, 292). Erik Eriksen, in discussing the cosmopolitan nature of the EU as a polity, refers to a 'sense of justice' as one where actors 'subject their actions to the constraints of a higher ranking law' out of a sense of duty and obligation to it. He continued that '[i]n order to ensure justice at the world level, or at least to be able to sanction norm breaches such as human rights violations and crimes against humanity, there is a need for a system that lays down the law, equally binding on all' (2006, 253). He continued: 'unlike what is often believed, [this approach to law] implies the need for coercive means because only with the threat of sanctions can the law compel compliance' (252). The presupposition here of course is that international law defined in this way has the universal moral robustness to legitimise such coercion and the EU has right on its side when it compels such compliance by virtue of what it is. Eriksen continues:

> I suggest as a criterion of a legitimate foreign policy that the EU does not aspire to become a world organization – a world state – but subscribes to the principles of human rights, democracy and rule of law also for dealing with international affairs, hence underscoring the cosmopolitan law of the people. (2006, 256)

Quoting from Tony Honoré, Eriksen continues that '[e]ven angels need "a system of laws in order to know the right thing to do"' (256). That this law of the people was devised in Europe and is exported by Europeans seems not to matter. Finally, this equation of right with the rule of law epitomises the neo-colonial nature of liberalism.

Elsewhere, references to justice in the academic literature on the EU as an ethical actor tend to fall back on the EU's declaration that social justice is at the heart of its policy and, as in the EU documentation, the concept tends to be alluded to only to be left undefined (see, e.g., Aggestam and Hill 2008, 102; Lerch and Schwellnus 2006, 315, 316; Manners 2002, 241). Even arch-realists are not uncomfortable with using the term, but defining justice seems to elicit less enthusiasm. Adrian Hyde-Price, for example, has argued that even a calculating and rational EU should not 'remain indifferent to gross human rights violations, international aggression or shocking manifestations of social and economic injustice' (2008, 36). But how would we know an instance of economic injustice when we see one? Do we revert to legal benchmarking or a sense of moral indignation? As the contemporary European fiscal crisis has shown, there were very few laws broken in the original collapse, but the injustices felt by the populations of Greece and elsewhere are innumerable. Is it right that technocrats be appointed by the EU to govern Italy and Greece? Is violent protest legitimately criminalised?

The neo-Kantianism expressed in EU foreign policy is also implicitly and sometimes explicitly neo-colonial. Where classical imperialism involved the control of territories at a distance, and Marxist-Leninist theories saw imperialism as economically driven, neo-Kantian imperialism is juridical (Anghie 2005). The extension of the regimes of international law, through such institutions as sovereignty, protectorates, colonial administration and so forth was structurally iniquitous and can hardly be equated with justice. The consequence today is that the structural barriers preventing most from being the architects of their own legal institutions are formidable, but those preventing popular control of global legal frameworks are simply out of sight. From the adoption of the *aquis communitaire* to the negotiation of the Common Agricultural Policy at the WTO, it is elite rather than popular participation that shapes the global institutional architecture and the virtues that come to shape global order are those promoted by these very same elites. Equating justice with the rule of law disempowers those who would articulate protest in the language of social justice by criminalising them as rule-breakers. The problem with critical accounts of EU foreign policy, those accounts that seek to evaluate the EU's actions beyond its borders, is that they have ceded the debate around questions of justice to the neo-Kantians. In the following section I focus on the work of Ian Manners to illustrate this point in more detail.

Virtue Ethics and EU Foreign Policy

My aim in this final section is twofold. First, I use virtue ethics as an analytical framework to dissect and critique perhaps the dominant account of the EU as a normative power. Second, I use this account to set out a more effective means of evaluating the EU's foreign policy. My focus is the work of Ian Manners. It is my claim that, in spite of concerted attempts by Manners to move beyond the implicit 'neo-colonialism' of Duchene's 'civilian power Europe' and the purported 'essentialism' of theories of ethical foreign policy (Whitman 2011, 4), by ultimately defending a neo-Kantian theory of justice, Manners repeats both flaws and reifies the EU.

Manners argued that the EU's normative power derived from its ability to persuade third-party and accession countries to accept its norms of behaviour through 'ideational' rather than 'material' means – through accepting the EU as a model of behaviour rather than have the EU dictate behaviour by force. Surveying the evolution of the EU and the adoption of the *aquis* by accession states, as well as the successful campaign against the death penalty worldwide, Manners concluded that '[t]he EU has gone further towards making its external relations informed by, and conditional on, a catalogue of norms' (Manners 2002, 241) and that these norms are both liberal and contagious. The sorts of norms Manners discussed were the principles of liberty, human rights, the rule of law, inclusive democracy, social solidarity and sustainable development, all principles set out by the EU in the Charter of Fundamental Freedoms. (Manners 2002, 242). From this set of observations Manners argued for a conception of the EU as a 'normative power' and defined it thus:

> The concept of normative power is an attempt to suggest that not only is the EU constructed on a normative basis, but importantly that this predisposes it to act in a normative way in world politics. It is built on the crucial, and usually overlooked observation that the most important factor shaping the international role of the EU is not what it does or what it says, *but what it is*. (Manners 2002, 252)

However, as critics have shown, not only is it unclear what the EU *is*, even by Manners' criteria, but being a norm entrepreneur is hardly unique to the EU. For example, Diez (2005) argued that Manners' framing of the concept of 'normative' specifies little that is unique to the EU and can equally be used to describe the United States, a state that Manners understands to be a quintessential 'hard power' in world politics. But why are the norms the EU promotes of any *moral* value? To answer this question Manners needed a theory of ethics that was largely absent in wider discussions of the subject. As the above discussion has sought to show, the meta-ethics of these debates are implicitly or explicitly Kantian, and Manners is no exception (Manners 2008a, 2008b).

Manners' aim in this second stage of his analysis was to move away from descriptive analysis to 'focus ... on the ways in which we might judge the normative ethics of the EU in world politics by critically discussing the principles that it seeks to promote, the practices through which it promotes them, and the impact they have' (Manners 2008a, 45). His aim is *not* to provide new ethical underpinnings for EU normative power, but to use ethics as formalised systems of moral philosophy to *evaluate and assess* EU behaviour. Manners distinguishes between virtue ethics, deontology and consequentialism, or 'living by example', 'being reasonable' and 'doing least harm' respectively (Manners 2008a, 59). Here, ethics, the branch of moral philosophy that formalises 'the study of the concepts involved in practical reasoning: good, right, duty, obligation, virtue, freedom, rationality, choice', (Blackburn 1996, 126), is used as descriptive and evaluative taxonomy. In short, Manners suggests that deontology, virtue ethics and consequentialism can each be used to help us 'judge' the EU's 'principles, actions and impact', arguing that 'we must judge the EU's creative efforts to promote a more just, cosmopolitical world in terms of its principles, actions and impact' (Manners 2008a, 47). The future, it seems, is given, what needs evaluating is the way in which the EU seeks to bring it about.

The problem is that, by arguing that maxims are the means through which this evaluation must take place, not only is the measuring instrument Kantian, but so are the 'cosmopolital' results Manners wishes to realise. What is also quite striking here is how Manners transforms each of these quite irreconcilable systems of ethics into Kantian, deontological *maxims*. Manners argues that deontology, consequentialism and virtue ethics each 'provide[s] the EU with *maxims which should shape the EU's normative power in world politics*' (Manners 2008a, 47, emphasis added). Surely only Kantian deontologists would subscribe to such a position, because only deontologists subscribe to the idea that moral maxims (that can be embedded in law) can or should guide behaviour at all. It is also symptomatic of a wider confusion that Manners also claims that Elizabeth Anscombe, the progenitor of modern-day virtue ethics, is the progenitor of consequentialism, a term she in fact coined to describe a system of ethics she thought fundamentally unsuited to politics (Manners 2008a, 58; cf. Anscombe 1958).

What are the analytical and practical implications of all of this? First, for the EU, justice is equated with law. This is problematic, particularly if one were to try and develop an account of the injustice of EU law. Second, with few academics moving this debate away from the EU's general framing, it seems the EU-watchers are working within the same liberal ideological parameters. From this perspective, everything looks Kantian – problems and solutions alike. This is problematic since, if the EU and scholars of the EU wish to achieve ends that are not neo-colonial, and nor do we wish to reify or essentialise the EU, then a change in the tenor of the debate is necessary. Third, and related to this, despite being favourably disposed towards virtue ethics, Manners' analysis ends up taking us back to neo-Kantianism and is unhelpful in moving this debate forward in a substantive way. Not only is the EU essentialised and given its own irreversible telos, but so too the cosmopolitical project it heralds is arguably neo-colonial. There is an alternative and it should, by now, be coming into view. It is not the law, but the virtues the EU espouses that should form the benchmark against which EU agents can and ought to be evaluated.

Conclusion: The Virtues of Virtue Ethics for the Study of EU Foreign Policy

Four things need to be borne in mind. From the perspective on virtue ethics developed here, institutions cannot be expected to be virtuous, only individuals can. Second, justice as a virtue is far more expansive than the realisation of the rule of law. Third, there are no transcendent virtues, only practice-virtues that are embedded and realised in time and space, by individuals and the groups they form and through institutions that often, if not always, undermine them. Fourth, I have argued that Kantian or neo-Kantian approaches to ethics tend towards a neo-colonial politics. I have argued that the equation of right with rule-following also tends to absolve responsibility and reifies the law. MacIntyre's approach to virtue ethics provides a valuable alternative to help us rethink ethics in this context. MacIntyre argues that virtues and practices are mutually sustaining, that institutions routinely undermine the virtues upheld by groups and individuals and that no moral claim is therefore independent of its sociological and historical context. It is this vital final point that is of most importance to the study of EU foreign policy. It is not that, as Eriksen would have it, we need the law so as to know what to do, but rather that we should have confidence in our stock of moral learning and take succour from our individual contexts. All moral beliefs are beliefs from a particular position and the virtue ethics approach provides a framework and language for defending non-rule-based accounts of ethics.

From MacIntyre's perspective, the EU as an institution can be expected consistently to contradict the moral and ethical standards it upholds. Second, however, we cannot hold 'the EU' to account, but must, rather, hold key individuals and groups to account in their respective roles and within the practices they defend, while judging them according to the virtues they proclaim, and also those that we bring to bear anew. As institutions develop in time, we should not be surprised that the EU, a technocratic institution at its core, is struggling to realise the virtues of democracy and social justice. Finally, we cannot assume that the principles the EU promotes are potentially universal. If, as it has been argued here, all moral claims are claims that are in reality sociologically and historically contingent, universalist claims are implicitly or explicitly neo-colonial. So, for example, one does not have to be a realist to heed E.H. Carr's calls for circumspection when we hear claims that the EU is promoting universal values of freedom and peace, since these claims are not unconnected to the EU's attempts to assert itself in the world, nor are these projects unconnected to the historical legacy of colonialism which has prepared the world for liberal values by making the world in the EU's own image. What does this say to alternative visions of the future, when liberal visions of world politics are taken for granted and the means by which we might assess them are said to lie in an internal assessment of the EU's ability to align with its own principles. This would make the EU judge and jury in its own trial and we would simply be holding liberalism to account on its own terms. Ian Manners puts it like this:

> The creative efforts and longer-term vision of EU normative power towards the achievement of a more just, cosmopolitical world which empowers people in the actual conditions of their lives should and must be based on more universally accepted values and principles that can be explained to both Europeans and non-European alike. (Manners 2008a, 60)

There is no question that the empowerment of individuals and groups 'in the actual conditions of their lives' is of singular political importance today. But, from this perspective no such 'universally accepted values and principles' exist, nor does the export of such and such values from the technocratic or intellectual heart of Europe 'to Europeans and non-Europeans alike' constitute anything more than neo-colonialism. As there are no transcendent grounds for adjudicating between the virtues, tolerance and humility become the supreme virtues when dealing with 'outsiders', and hubris the supreme vice.

In this paper, I have argued that this vision of virtue ethics can provide both a critical and constructive account of EU foreign policy. In particular, I have criticised the equation of law with justice and the assumed correspondence between the following of rules with right moral behaviour prevalent in both the policy and academic commentary on EU foreign policy. These predominantly neo-Kantian ways of understanding EU foreign policy tend towards neo-imperialism and ought to be avoided, since, if the EU seeks to act as a third-party mediator and actor in external conflicts, it cannot presume, by virtue of establishing the rules and by virtue of *what it claims to be*, to have justice on its side. Using insights taken from virtue ethics, I argued for an approach to evaluating the EU based on the idea that justice is relative to the virtues that we pursue in our daily lives, and that these virtues can only be properly understood in relation to the practices through which they are realised and the institutions we build to defend them. I argued that we need to disaggregate the EU's institutions and the practices of key officials and the virtues they promote or defend. I illustrated the theoretical value of this approach through a concrete intervention in debates surrounding whether the EU is a 'normative power' or not. This outline suggests a radical departure from the norm, and it is hoped that this discussion provides food for thought and can contribute to further invigorating and more empirically oriented research programmes along these lines.

Acknowledgements

This paper was researched and written under the auspice of the EU 7th Framework Programme. Project title: 'Building a Just and Durable Peace by Piece' (no. 217488). For more information, visit Email:www.justpeace.se. A shorter version of this paper appeared in *CFSP Forum* (7/2, 2009). I am grateful to the editors for their comments on this earlier draft. The arguments of this paper have also benefited greatly from insightful comments and constructive criticism from Kirsten Ainley, Chris Brown, Joe Hoover, Adrian Hyde-Price, Ana Juncos, Nieves Perez-Solorzano and Karen Smith. I am also grateful for the critical comments from participants at the 'Just and Durable Peace by Piece' regional seminar in Sarajevo, and the European Governance Research Group, University of Bristol, where an earlier draft of this paper was presented.

Note

[1] This approach is quite distinct from a system of ethics that derives 'the good' from the degree to which actions contribute to aggregate happiness, or a relativist position that sees no transcendent grounds on which to build moral claims. Consequentialism does not feature in this paper in any meaningful way, but will be left for a separate treatment. While there is an extensive literature on the so-called 'logic of consequences' (e.g. March and Olsen 1989), there is little in this literature that is concerned with consequentialism and utilitarianism as a grounding for ethics. Rather, it is more generally used as an explanatory tool for identifying an ideal type of rational agency, one juxtaposed with a 'logic of appropriateness' – action consciously or unconsciously related to rule-following. In both instances the 'normative' is stripped down to a level consistent with contemporary social scientific standards of objectivity and the prior meta-ethical discussions as to the morality of rule following or of consequences as a criterion for right is elided. Using these two logics as explanatory tools is another example of a problem I identify here, but my focus will be on Kantian and neo-Kantian thought.

References

Aggestam, L. 2008. "Introduction: Ethical Power Europe?" *International Affairs* 84 (1): 1–11.

Aggestam, L., and C. Hill. 2008. "The Challenge of Multiculturalism in European Foreign Policy." *International Affairs* 84 (1): 97–114.

Anghie, A. 2005. *Imperialism, Sovereignty, and the Making of International Law*. Cambridge: Cambridge University Press.

Anscombe, Elizabeth. 1958. "Modern Moral Philosophy." *Philosophy* 33 (124): 1–19.

Barry, B. M. 1995. *Justice as Impartiality*. Oxford: Clarendon Press.

Behnke, A. 2008. "'Eternal Peace' as the Graveyard of the Political: A Critique of Kant's Zum Ewigen Frieden." *Millennium – Journal of International Studies* 36 (3): 513–531.

Bicchi, F. 2006. 'Our size fits all': normative power Europe and the Mediterranean" *Journal of European Public Policy* 13 (2): 286–303.

Blackburn, S. 1996. *Oxford Dictionary of Philosophy*. Oxford: Oxford University Press.

Blackledge, Paul, and Neil Davidson, eds. 2008. *Alasdair Macintyre's Engagement with Marxism: Selected Writings 1953–1974*. Leiden: Brill.

Brown, C. 2010 [1999]. "Towards a Neo-Aristotelian Resolution of the Cosmopolitan-Communitarian Debate." In *Practical Judgement in International Political Theory: Selected Essays*, edited by Chris Brown, 72–89. London: Routledge.

Chandler, D. 2004. "Imposing the 'Rule of Law': the Lessons of BiH for Peacebuilding in Iraq." *International Peacekeeping* 11 (2): 312–333.

Chandler, D. 2006. *Empire in Denial: The Politics of State-Building*. London: Pluto.

Crisp, R. 1996. *How Should one Live? Essays on the Virtues*. Oxford: Clarendon.

Crossley-Frolick, K. A. 2011. The European Union and transitional justice: human rights and post-conflict reconciliation in Europe and beyond. *Contemporary Readings in Law and Social Justice* 1 (1): 33–57.

Diez, T. 2005. "Constructing the Self and Changing Others: Reconsidering Normative Power Europe Millennium." *Journal of International Studies* 33 (3): 613–636.

Diez, T., and M. Pace. 2011. "Normative Power Europe and Conflict Transformation." In *Normative Power Europe: Empirical and Theoretical Perspectives*, edited by R. G. Whitman, 210–225. Houndmills, Basingstoke; New York: Palgrave Macmillan.

Doyle, M. 1983. "Kant, Liberal Legacies, and Foreign Affairs." *Philosophy and Public Affairs* 12 (3): 205–235.

Doyle, M. W. 1986. "Liberalism and World Politics." *American Political Science Review* 80 (4): 1151–1169.

Eriksen, E. O. 2006. "The EU – A Cosmopolitan Polity?" *Journal of European Public Policy* 13 (2): 252–269.

European Commission. 2004. *Freedom, Security and Justice for All: Justice and Home Affairs in the European Union*. Brussels:.

European Commission. 2009. *Underwriting Justice for All*. Brussels:. Accessed February 17, 2009. http://ec.eu ropa.eu/europeaid/what/governance-democracy/justice/index_en.htm (link no longer operative).

European Commission. 2010. *The EU Charter of Fundamental Rights*. Brussels:.

European Council. 2003. *A Secure Europe in a Better World. European Security Strategy*. Brussels:.

Fukuyama, Francis. 1989. "The End of History?" *The National Interest* 16: 3–18.

Gaskarth, J. 2011. "Where Would We Be Without Rules? A Virtue Ethics Approach to Foreign Policy Analysis." *Review of International Studies* 37 (1): 393–415.

Gaskarth, J. 2012. "The Virtues in International Society." *European Journal of International Relations* 18 (3): 431–453.

Habermas, J. 1990. *Moral Consciousness and Communicative Action*. Cambridge: Polity.

Horton, J., and S. Mendus. 1994. *After MacIntyre: Critical Perspectives on the Work of Alasdair MacIntyre*. Cambridge: Polity.

Hurrell, A. 1990. "Kant and the Kantian paradigm in international relations." *European Journal of International Relations* 16 (3): 183–205.

Hyde-Price, A. 2008. "A 'tragic actor'? A Realist Perspective on 'Ethical Power Europe'." *International Affairs* 84 (1): 29–44.

Jahn, B. 2000. *The Cultural Construction of International Relations: The Invention of the State of Nature*. Basingstoke: Macmillan.

Jahn, I. 2005. *Kant, Mill, and Illiberal Legacies in International Affairs*. International Organization 59 (01): 177–207.

Jahn, I. 2009. *Liberal Internationalism: From Ideology to Empirical Theory – and Back Again*. International Theory 1 (03): 409–438.

Juncos, AnaE. 2011. "Power Discourses and Power Practices: The EU's Role as a Normative Power in Bosnia." In *Normative Power Europe: Empirical and Theoretical Perspectives*, edited by R. G. Whitman, 83–102. Houndmills, Basingstoke; New York: Palgrave Macmillan.

Juncos, AnaE. 2013. *EU Foreign and Security Policy in Bosnia: The Politics of Coherence and Effectiveness*. Manchester: Manchester University Press.

Kagan, Robert. 2002. "Power and Weakness." *Policy Review*, Issue 113, June, Accessed April 14, 2011. http://www.hoover.org/publications/policy-review/5136

Kant, I. 1964. *Groundwork of the Metaphysic of Morals*. New York: Harper and Row.

Kant, I. 1991a. "The Metaphysics of Morals." In *Kant: Political writings*, edited by H. Reiss, 131–175. Cambridge: Cambridge University Press.

Kant, I. 1991b. "Idea for a Universal History with a Cosmopolitan Purpose." In *Kant: Political Writings*, edited by H. Reiss, 41–53. Cambridge: Cambridge University Press.

Kant, I. 1991c. "Perpetual Peace: A Philosophical Sketch (H. B. Nisbet, Trans.)." In *Kant: Political Writings*, edited by H. Reiss. 2nd ed., 93–130. Cambridge: Cambridge University Press.

Kant, I. 1993. *Critique of Pure Reason*. London: J.M. Dent.

Lerch, M., and G. Schwellnus. 2006. "Normative by Nature? The Role of Coherence in Justifying the EU's External Human Rights Policy." *Journal of European Public Policy* 13 (2): 304–321.

Linklater, A. 2011. *The problem of harm in world politics: theoretical investigations*. Cambridge: Cambridge University Press.

MacIntyre, A. 1981. *After Virtue: A Study in Moral Theory*. London: Duckworth.

MacIntyre, A. 1988. *Whose Justice? Which Rationality?* Notre Dame, Indiana: University of Notre Dame Press.

Mani, R. 2002. *Beyond Retribution: Seeking Justice in the Shadows of War.* Cambridge: Polity Press.

Mani, R. 2005. "Rebuilding an Inclusive Political Community After War." *Security Dialogue* 36 (4): 511–526.

Manners, I. 2002. "Normative Power Europe: A Contradiction in Terms?" *JCMS* 40 (2): 235–258.

Manners, I. 2006. "The European Union as a Normative Power: A Response to Thomas Diez." *Millennium – Journal of International Studies* 35 (1): 167–180.

Manners, I. 2008a. "The Normative Ethics of the European Union." *International Affairs* 84 (1): 45–60.

Manners, Ian. 2008b. "Normative Power Europe: A Transdisciplinary Approach to European Studies." In *Handbook of European studies,* edited by Chris Rumford, 561–586. London: Sage.

March, J. G., and J. P., Olsen, 1989. *Rediscovering Institutions: The Organizational Basis of Politics.* New York: Free Press.

Marks, G., L. Hooghe, and K. Blank. 1996. "European Integration from the 1980s: State-Centric v. Multi-level Governance." *Journal of Common Market Studies* 34 (3): 341–378.

Nardin, T. 2006. "International Political Theory and the Question of Justice." *International Affairs* 82 (3): 449–465.

Pace, M. 2007. "The construction of EU Normative Power." *JCMS* 45: 1041–1064.

Paris, R. 2004. *At War's End: Building Peace After Civil Conflict.* Cambridge: Cambridge University Press.

Rawls, J. 1971. *A Theory of Justice.* Oxford: Oxford University Press.

Richmond, O. P. 2006. "The Problem of Peace: Understanding the 'Liberal Peace'." *Conflict, Security, Development* 6 (3): 291–314.

Rosen, A. D. 1993. *Kant's Theory of Justice.* London: Cornell University Press.

Scheipers, Sibylle, and Daniela Sicurelli. 2007. "Normative Power Europe: A Credible Utopia?." *JCMS: Journal of Common Market Studies* 45 (2): 435–457.

Sriram, C. L. 2007. "Justice as Peace? Liberal Peacebuilding and Strategies of Transitional Justice." *Global Society* 21 (4): 579–591.

Tsakatika, M. 2008. *Political Responsibility and the European Union.* Manchester: University of Manchester Press.

Tuck, R. 2001. *The Rights of War and Peace: Political Thought and the International Order From Grotius to Kant.* Oxford: Oxford University Press.

Walzer, M. 1992. *Just and Unjust Wars: A Moral Argument with Historical Illustrations.* London: BasicBooks.

Whitman, R. G.. 2011b. "Norms, Power and Europe: A New Agenda for the Study of the EU." In *Normative Power Europe: Empirical and Theoretical Perspectives,* ed. Richard G. Whitman, 1–24. Houndmills, Basingstoke: Palgrave.

Wight, C. 2006. *Agents, Structures and International Relations: Politics as Ontology.* Cambridge: Cambridge University Press.

Informal Governance and the Eurozone Crisis

ALEXANDRA HENNESSY

Seton Hall University, USA

ABSTRACT   *Europe's sovereign debt crisis has left no doubt that Germany has the ultimate authority in financial matters in the EU. However, between 2009 and 2012 Germany has been unable to safeguard its core objectives, which we define as follows: (1) stabilizing the eurozone; (2) limiting the taxpayers' financial guarantee exposure; and (3) keeping inflation low. This outcome is at odds with the expectation of the informal governance literature that the dominant country will always be able to protect its core interests after overriding the ordinary procedure. We argue that Germany's quandary can be explained by two interrelated factors. First, policymakers were subject to an incentive structure that encouraged crisis mitigation efforts, but not preparedness. This explains Germany's long hesitation before offering any assistance to its partners. Second, once financial guarantees were provided, political disagreements over the sequence of reform steps as well as instruments and conditionality of financial assistance programmes prolonged investor fears of a eurozone breakup, further compromising Germany's interests.*

Introduction

A rich literature on flexibility in international organizations has shown that occasional violations of formal rules are tolerated when the costs of compliance are excessive (Koremenos, Lipson, and Snidal 2001; Rosendorff and Milner 2001; Rosendorff 2005; Koremenos 2005). Stone's (2011) work has been particularly insightful by demonstrating that dominant states can renegotiate the rules of international organizations in informal ways when the costs of adhering to legal rule revision procedures are prohibitive. In ordinary times, international institutions generate predictable policies that reflect the distribution of formal influence among their members, but when the dominant players perceive the content of treaties as harmful they may override existing rules to safeguard their core interests (Stone 2011).

However, this research also raises new puzzles. This paper highlights the inability of the informal governance literature to explain why hegemons may be unable to safeguard their core interests, despite the capability to override the formal procedure. The very definition of 'hegemon' suggests that the dominant agent should always be able to impose its will on other members in the system. Yet, if the dominant agent is confronted with time-inconsistency problems, an override of the formal procedure may not yield a satisfactory solution to the problem that gave rise to informal governance in the first place. It has been shown that some leaders impose short-term costs to mitigate long-term problems, while others merely choose to delay the pain (Pierson 2004; Jacobs 2011). If the dominant country is faced with a crisis that requires high upfront costs, but responds to an incentive structure that rewards delay, the hegemon may be unable to protect its core interests. Initial emergency measures may constrain future moves in ways that can cause the top dog to lose out in the distributive struggle. Conflicting interests over the sequence of policy change, as well as instruments and conditionality of crisis-fighting measures may leave the dominant actor unable to exploit the benefits of informal governance. Thus, to understand why a dominant country may be unable to safeguard its core objectives, it is important to analyze the incentive structure policymakers react to and how previous moves may constrain the hegemon's subsequent room of manoeuvre.

This paper uses the example of the eurozone sovereign debt crisis to show why the dominant country may be unable to protect its core interests. The eurozone debt crisis has left no doubt that Germany has the ultimate authority over financial matters in the EU. This outcome is consistent with Stone's (2011) view of power in the EU. What is puzzling is that, between 2009 and 2012, Germany proved incapable of using its political and economic resources to satisfy key domestic and foreign policy ends, which we define as follows: (1) stabilizing the eurozone; (2) limiting the taxpayers' financial guarantee exposure; and (3) keeping inflation low. Germany's foreign policy after the end of the Cold War was driven by the idea that a united Germany would reassure other states of its peaceful intentions by being firmly embedded in European institutions. But as agents for the taxpayers, reelection-seeking officials understandably considered it their duty to limit the financial risks domestic constituents assume for other countries. Berlin's strong commitment to price stability is rooted in the experience with inflationary processes in the 1920s, and the European Central Bank (ECB) was modeled after the German Bundesbank because of the latter's success in keeping inflation rates under control.

According to the informal governance perspective, Germany's authority as creditor-in-chief, stability anchor and growth engine in the EU should have enabled political officials to safeguard these objectives. Yet, the rising price tag of eurozone rescue programmes foiled the goal of limiting taxpayers' financial guarantee burden. The ECB has injected more than 1 trillion euros into the financial system, although it lacks the authority to purchase sovereign debt from troubled states. German inflation is expected to rise as a result of the structural adjustments the peripheral member states are making. And in spite of manifold rescue measures, the break-up of the eurozone was considered a real possibility by financial market participants, policymakers and EU officials. We argue that Germany's failure to safeguard its core interests can be explained by two interrelated factors. First, policymakers were subject to an incentive structure that encouraged crisis mitigation efforts, but not preparedness. This explains Germany's long hesitation before offering any assistance to its partners. Second, once financial guarantees were provided, political disagreements over sequence of reform steps as well as instruments and conditionality of financial assistance programmes prolonged investor fears of a eurozone breakup. Since the price for calming financial markets tends to rise as the market panic increases, the government gradually sacrificed the objective of limiting the taxpayers' financial guarantee exposure.

It is not this paper's goal to challenge Stone's model; least of all with a single case study. But the discussion of an anomalous case presents an opportunity to refine the informal governance theory by explicating the circumstances under which the dominant country can lose out in the distributive struggle within the international institution, despite the capacity to override the formal procedure. Since the debt turmoil is the most severe eurozone crisis to date, it constitutes an important case that sheds light on incentives to cooperate within the EU during shock times.

This article is also an attempt to build a bridge between comparative politics studies and international relations perspectives on the debt crisis. Scholarship with a comparative perspective has productively located the origins of the turmoil in the euro's birth defects (the absence of economic and political union), but no efforts have been made to explain the EU's failure to stabilize the eurozone. International relations scholars, on the other hand, have refused to engage with the debt crisis, despite the field's longstanding concern with economic crises, incentives for international cooperation and the effectiveness of international institutions.[1]

In what follows, I first describe the core interests Germany sought to protect during the debt drama. The subsequent section identifies the incentive structure that explains Germany's long hesitation before providing any financial assistance. I then explicate how member state disagreements over the sequence of reform steps as well as instruments, scope and conditionality of financial assistance programmes maintained investor fears of a eurozone breakup. The final section concludes with a review of the findings and a discussion of the implications.

Germany's Core Interests

A Stable Eurozone

Throughout the post-World War II period, a strong commitment to EU integration has been a matter of national interest for Germany. German chancellors were frequently willing to subordinate domestic interests to greater European integration (Heisenberg 2006). Although European citizens remain primarily attached to their nation-state and some harbour scepticism towards certain EU projects, the notion of a European identity is very strong in Germany and support for the EU is high (Fligstein 2008, 157). Policymakers wanted eurozone entry to be irrevocable, and therefore spelled out no path to exit. When the Greek debt crisis threatened to wreck the entire system, German policymakers treated the defence of the eurozone as a fundamental national interest. The government's message was that a broken eurozone would not only threaten Germany's economic interests, but more than half a century of European integration, the anchor for German foreign policy. Shortly before a vote on eurozone rescue measures, Angela Merkel told the German Parliament: 'If the euro fails, Europe fails. That's why the most important goal for the government must be that Europe emerges stronger from the crisis. This means Europe must become a stability union.'[2]

Limiting the Taxpayers' Financial Guarantee Exposure

Germany agreed to provide financial assistance programmes for its partners, but political incumbents understandably considered it their duty to limit the risks for the German taxpayer. The Maastricht criteria and Stability and Growth Pact had been designed to commit the member states to fiscal discipline, and Article 125 of the Lisbon treaty was supposed to preclude bailout-outs of other member states. However, a rigid enforcement of the acquis communautaire in the wake of the upheaval would have been politically unacceptable and systemically threatening to the eurozone and even the EU itself. Rifts in the German Bundestag, but also within the governing coalition, over the size and conditionality of bailouts and financial guarantee programmes reflect the difficulty of justifying this kind of solidarity to domestic constituents, despite the pro-EU attitude in the country and competitive export sector that benefited from the common currency.

Low Inflation Rates

Securing low inflation rates has been central to German monetary policy in the post-World War II period, as inflationary developments have been associated with the impoverishment and radicalization of the middle class, the triumph of National Socialism, and the demise of the Weimar Republic. The Bundesbank was created with the primary objective to maintain price stability. Other countries that have long had relatively dependent central banks, such as Britain, Ireland and France, were more tolerant of inflation than high unemployment levels (Hall and Franzese 1998). The ECB was modeled after the Bundesbank because of the latter's independence and focus on price stability (Alesina and Grilli 1991). While other central banks, such as the Bank of England and the US Federal Reserve, regularly carry out large-scale purchases of sovereign bonds, EU treaties have been interpreted to prohibit this practice. In addition, the ECB does not have a strong financial-stability mandate that could justify intervention to prevent turmoil on the bond markets.

Core Interests and Incentive Structures

How did Germany's core interests translate into actions? In ordinary times, the distribution of power in the EU is relatively flat, legal procedures defuse conflicts (Thomson et al. 2006), and Berlin's preferred mode of presenting EU initiatives is in cooperation with France (Stone 2011, ch. 6). During business-as-usual negotiations, the EU countries often rely on the agenda-setting powers of the European Commission (Princen 2009; Hennessy 2011) or the Council presidency (Tallberg 2006; Kleine 2012) to adjudicate between divergent member state demands. However, the debt crisis constituted a major shock that affected the core interests of both strong and weak member states, pushing a reluctant Germany into the role of hegemon (Paterson 2011; Matthijs and Blyth 2011).

Procedural approaches modeling the legal sequence of EU decision making offer little purchase on explaining Germany's quandary as rule violations occurred on an unprecedented scale: the no-bailout clause of the Lisbon Treaty (Article 125) was voided through fiscal transfers to debt-ridden member states. The ECB conducted several long-term refinancing operations although it lacks the authority to purchase sovereign debt from troubled states. The International Monetary Fund (IMF) has shifted its emphasis from providing balance of payments support to offering budgetary support, which is illegal. The Copenhagen Criteria, which specify that member states must preserve democratic governance, have been brushed aside by the installation of caretaker governments in Greece, Italy and Spain. Representatives of the European Commission, ECB and IMF have monitored the implementation of austerity programmes in recipient countries, stripping them of budgetary sovereignty. Emergency measures and institutional change were crucially shaped by Germany, while EU officials took the back seat. It is therefore more fruitful to analyze the options available to German policymakers, the incentive structure they reacted to, and how core interests translated into eurozone rescue measures and eventually caused Germany to sacrifice its core interests.

If fundamental preferences were fully deterministic, German officials would have provided credible backstops for the large eurozone economies right after the Greek debt crisis became acute in late 2009 and pursued steps towards fiscal and banking union all at once. This claim relies on a counterfactual that can never be proven. However, there are reasons to believe that an alternative crisis management could have eliminated self-fulfilling expectations of contagion. Specifically, instantaneous financial guarantees for the EU's large economies may have stabilized the eurozone sooner, and more cost-effectively, than two and a half years of ad hoc emergency measures that kept investors guessing about redenomination risk.[3] Gray (2009) has demonstrated that the EU can send strong signals to financial markets about the trajectory of a particular country. Closing negotiation chapters on domestic economic policy (receiving a seal of approval from Brussels) substantially decreases perceptions of default risk in those countries. This means that the EU can confer investor confidence that domestic economic reforms alone cannot accomplish.

However, EU mandated rescue measures will be tested when market participants doubt their effectiveness. Financial crises can be driven by economic fundamentals, but the actual trigger may be the beliefs of financial market participants (Krugman 1996). In this sort of environment, investor expectations about government actions have an important feedback in determining what those actions should be. Once self-fulfilling expectations coalesce around a crisis outcome, it will be extremely difficult for policymakers to enforce their preferred equilibrium. This dynamic entails a potential for contagion that need not have occurred but does so because market participants expect it to (Obstfeld 1994). Gartner and Griesbach (2012) found evidence that Europe's sovereign debt crisis has been driven mainly by self-fulfilling forces.

Undoubtedly, the provision of sizeable backstops for Spain and Italy would have increased German taxpayers' financial guarantee exposure as well. Fiscal and banking union take time to implement and would have required legal changes. However, rule violations between 2009 and 2012 were ubiquitous, and deeper fiscal integration became a reality with the Greek bailouts, the creation of a European rescue fund, and surveillance of austerity programmes by the troika.[4] In June 2012, the European Commission proposed a framework for establishing a banking union with centralized powers to supervise banks and plans for sharing the costs of recapitalizing cross-border banks. The point is that an instantaneous commitment to deeper integration would have sent a more convincing signal to financial markets than limited, piecemeal emergency measures. Credible backstops in the immediate aftermath of the turmoil would have alleviated the need for additional financial guarantees Berlin made available to several member states on the verge of losing capital market access. Whether such radical measures would have been politically feasible in the immediate aftermath of the Greek debt crisis will never be known, but weak competition in the electoral arena[5] and opposition parties urging more comprehensive rescue measures indicate that the government should have been able to incur higher upfront costs to shore up the bond markets of the large eurozone economies.

But German policymakers did not choose this route. Instead, they agreed to piecemeal emergency measures only after long periods of indecision and in contradiction to previous announcements, triggering contagion and creating a permanent state of emergency. Rising risk premiums for Greece, Ireland, Italy, Portugal, Spain and Cyprus, outflows of capital and bank deposits in Europe's periphery, and the threat of sovereign bankruptcies perpetuated investor fears of a eurozone breakup. German taxpayers have provided sizeable financial guarantees for other eurozone countries, and the Bundesbank is preparing to accept higher inflation rates. This means that, despite the renationalization of decision making and growth of executive powers, Germany was not capable of safeguarding its core interests.

We propose that this outcome is the result of policymakers responding to an incentive structure that encouraged crisis mitigation efforts rather than spending on preparedness. From the literature on natural disaster policy we know that political officials are not very good at investing in disaster preparedness (Healy and Malhotra 2009). Public policies are often characterized by short-sightedness and inefficiencies because politicians are incentivized to invest in policies that produce short-term benefits. In the same vein, political leaders lack incentives to invest in solving problems that appear manageable at first, but may cause escalating costs if they continue to fester. As agents for the taxpayers, political officials understandably consider it their duty to limit the financial risks of crisis resolution mechanisms. But this means that officials lack the mandate to implement costly and comprehensive measures as long as the costs of inaction seem bearable. If citizens are unaware of the potentially exploding costs of inaction they may punish officials for incurring large upfront costs to address the problem. Even if political incumbents had the foresight to avert a major crisis before it became acute, voters oblivious to the forestalled disaster might still punish incumbents for the immediate costs incurred to control the turmoil.

Domestic constituencies do not want elected officials to spend on crisis prevention before the disaster has occurred because it is impossible for citizens to observe the counterfactual: what would have been the impact of the turmoil in the absence of preparedness spending (Healy and Malhotra 2009). Conversely, spending money on mitigating a disaster is observable through the news media, and citizens can more easily reward or punish policymakers' crisis management skills.[6] Imminent re-election pressures often induce politicians to enact quick fixes with short-term benefits rather than more comprehensive measures that require higher upfront costs (Sobel and Leeson 2006).

The government's room for maneuver grows, however, as the costs of inaction or ineffective 'quick fixes' become visible and increasingly intolerable. Once citizens are convinced that the consequences of inaction will be harmful they will approve of drastic government intervention, but not before. While officials can still take corrective measures as the market panic increases, the price for calming financial markets will be higher (Featherstone 2011). By the time decision-makers finally obtain a mandate for investing in crisis resolution mechanisms, it may be too late if the costs of inaction have grown exponentially. Ironically, a delayed crisis management resulting from the desire to limit the financial risks for the taxpayer may in fact increase the fiscal outlays required to solve the problem.

Dilatory Crisis Management

The dynamics of Germany's crisis management between 2009 and 2012 indicate that government officials responded to such an incentive structure. Political incumbents provided financial assistance programs to debt-ridden member states, but only after the costs of inaction had become visible and increasingly intolerable. Limited financial guarantees were offered or augmented only after front-page headlines shrieked of rising government bond yields, sovereign downgrades by rating agencies, outflows of capital from weak banks, and an imminent eurozone breakup. The German government initially refused to provide financial assistance to Greece because such a move 'would be against the rules'. Germany eventually reached an agreement with France on a bailout package for Greece, but only in May 2010 – seven months after the Greek debt drama first shook European markets.

For the majority of German citizens, the first bailout was already a step too far. Figure 1 shows that the biggest drop in Angela Merkel's approval ratings occurred right after the first Greek bailout, from 1.8 points to 0.5 points. For many German citizens, bailing out another member state crossed the line into an unacceptable 'joint liability union'.

Media headlines conjured up images of lazy, corrupt, spendthrift Greeks as the villains who brought the eurozone to ruin (Jones 2010).[7] In February 2010, a survey showed that 53% of Germans wanted Greece to be kicked out of the eurozone.[8] The dire consequences of failing to address potential systemic risk, by contrast, were underrepresented in the media. However, Merkel's approval ratings recovered and even surpassed those of her opponents 17 months later, despite unpopular eurozone emergency measures for Greece, Ireland and Portugal.

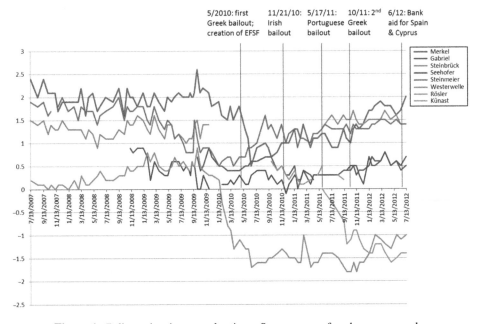

Figure 1. Policymakers' approval ratings. *Source*: www.forschungsgruppe.de.

In May 2010 the European Financial Stability Facility (EFSF) was created to provide financial assistance to euro area member states. After Germany had vowed to support Greece only once, Athens was soon unable to access capital markets, fueling concerns that Greece might have to default. Berlin bowed to international pressure to increase the size of the EFSF, but only in June 2011, after both Ireland and Portugal had been on the brink of losing access to capital markets. The EFSF is scheduled to be replaced with the permanent European Stability Mechanism (ESM), which will have a lending capacity of 500 billion euros.[9]

Figure 2 shows that, by June 2011, German citizens considered the eurozone debt crisis the most important problem facing their country. However, the perception that the eurozone crisis was a bigger challenge than, for example, high unemployment or shrinking public pension levels materialized only after Greece, Ireland and Portugal had received EFSF bailout funds and rumours about Greece requiring a second bailout had contributed to negative market sentiment. In October 2011 Greece received a second bailout, and policymakers reached a settlement with private banks on a 'voluntary' 50% reduction of Greece's debt in the hands of private investors.

Germany agreed to provide the lion's share of the bailouts and financial guarantees for its partners,[10] but these measures did not shore up the larger Spanish and Italian bond markets. As the full scale of Spain's weak banking sector gradually became apparent, financial market participants did not believe that Madrid could afford to guarantee 12% of EFSF resources. In June 2012, Spain was promised 100 billion euros in EFSF funds and Cyprus obtained 10 billion euros to shore up failing banks.[11] Since policymakers failed to put in place persuasive backstops, the eurozone breakup risk rose notably during the second half of 2011 and 2012. Consequently, the costs of stabilizing the eurozone have

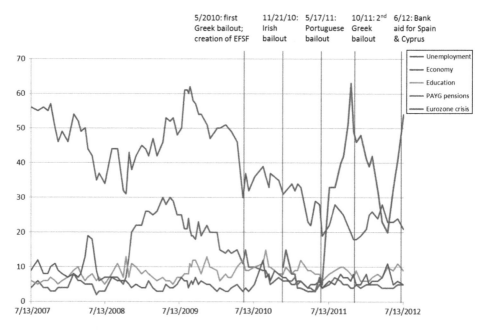

Figure 2. Most important challenges facing Germany. *Source*: www.forschungsgruppe.de.

grown steeply, compromising Germany's objective to limit the taxpayers' financial guarantee exposure.

Germany's piecemeal response to the sovereign debt crisis was criticized on several fronts. Poland's foreign minister declared that he feared German inaction more than German power.[12] Belgium's former prime minister complained in early 2012 that 'we are no nearer solving the crisis than in December 2009, when Greece's debt situation first became apparent'.[13] The German social democrats accused the governing coalition of taking a myopic view of Germany's interests in the effort to save the eurozone, but nonetheless voted with the conservative-liberal parties in support of every eurozone rescue measure. And the British chancellor suggested that German incumbents might be incentivized to enact short-sighted policies when he mentioned that a Greek exit could be necessary to convince German voters that it was worth spending more money on firewalls for other member states.[14]

Remarkably, neither the social democrats nor Eurosceptics in Merkel's own governing coalition were capable of using the eurozone crisis between 2009 and 2012 to their advantage. Although popular resentment toward sovereign bailouts ran deep, citizens consistently considered the Christian conservatives more competent in dealing with the debt crisis than the opposition social democrats, as Figure 3 shows.

In contrast to the limited, piecemeal rescue measures offered by the government, the social democrats had called for more comprehensive eurozone rescue measures early on. While the government's eurozone policies had failed to stabilize the eurozone and progressively increased taxpayers' financial guarantee load, the small-step approach evidently paid off in terms of Merkel's approval ratings and, ironically, her party's reputation as effective crisis manager. Although the Christian Democrats had to stomach electoral losses in several regional elections, particularly in the most populous state of

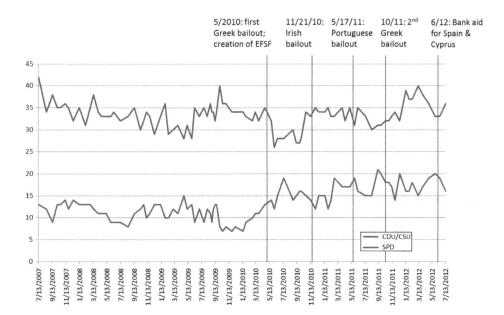

Figure 3. Political parties' economic policy competence. *Source*: www.forschungsgruppe.de.

North Rhine-Westphalia in May 2010 and May 2012, it was not the social democrats that benefited from disaffected Christian Democratic voters, but smaller political parties such as the greens and the pirate party.[15]

Disputes over the Sequence of Reform Steps

The peculiar incentive structure German policymakers faced explains the government's long hesitation before it agreed to offer financial assistance to troubled member states, but the failure to stabilize the eurozone after financial support was granted requires an examination of the sequence and process by which goals were pursued. It is well known that the negotiation processes generate their own stakes for the actors involved. A long 'shadow of the future' can inhibit cooperation by raising the stakes over which the actors are bargaining (Fearon 1995). Conversely, previous moves may shape future incentives for cooperation. Arguing hard against a particular solution is likely to increase the political costs of accepting that solution later in the game. Having yielded to pressure on previous occasions tends to increase the political costs of further concessions (Underdal 1992). In the EU, incentives to cooperate depend on the expected size of the reward and the likelihood that it will actually materialize before too long (Öhler, Nunnenkamp, and Dreher 2012, 140). If the rewards of EU agreements appear too distant, incentives to cooperate will weaken (Grabbe 2001). But cooperation will also be difficult to sustain if one state unexpectedly bears a larger share of the costs (Koremenos 2001, 2005).

Throughout the sovereign debt crisis, EU diplomacy was characterized by disputes over the sequence of reform steps as well as instruments, scope and conditionality of emergency measures. Permanent renegotiations of financial assistance programmes reflect a long shadow of the future in a high-stakes bargaining process. Once Germany had decided to offer financial guarantees to its partners, the succession of policy change became a source of contestation between the member states: before pooling debt liabilities with other countries, Berlin sought to pool control over economic policies and initiate concrete steps towards political union. However, peripheral member states demanded more solidarity before surrendering budgetary sovereignty.

In the eurozone's periphery, resentment grew over the quid pro quo Germany extracted in exchange for financial assistance programmes. Germany's contribution to the two Greek bailouts as well as financial guarantees provided through the EFSF were conditional on recipient governments implementing far-reaching austerity measures and structural reforms. In exchange for agreeing to make the temporary EFSF permanent, Germany insisted that all eurozone states adopt a fiscal pact that envisages automated, rather than negotiated, sanctions for violating fiscal discipline. The Pact also mandates the incorporation of a constitutional 'debt-brake' enforcing a balanced budget. The purpose was to ensure that more German support will not be pledged in guarantees to eurozone states without the strict budget discipline enshrined in the fiscal pact.

Yet, whenever a member state was on the brink of losing access to capital markets, Germany was under international pressure to provide more guarantees quickly, leaving lengthy treaty reforms for the period after the financial guarantees had already materialized. The EFSF and IMF made 78 billion euros available to Portugal in April 2011, and provided 85 billion euros to Ireland in November 2011, of which 35 billion will be used to recapitalize failing banks. Spain was promised 100 billion euros in EFSF, but failed to obtain direct capital injections for its failing banks. The full weakness of Spain's banks, which are loaded with bad real-estate investments, became apparent only gradually as Spain's national supervisor had repeatedly underestimated the amount a rescue would cost. Several reassessments of the total costs of a bailout reinforced investors' concerns that Spain might be next in line to seek a full sovereign bailout, prompting an angry response from the ECB president: 'There is a first assessment, then a second, a third, a fourth. This is the worst possible way of doing things. Everyone ends up doing the right thing, but at the highest cost.'[16]

Disputes over the sequence of crisis-fighting measures were particularly intense when member states negotiated assistance for the Spanish banks. Spain lobbied hard for the direct injection of eurozone rescue funds into Spanish banks in order to break the damaging feedback loop between weak sovereigns and weak banks. The ECB and policymakers in peripheral countries shared Spain's concern that EFSF funds channeled through the Spanish government would add to Madrid's debt, pushing the country towards a full-scale bailout that might eat up almost all of the eurozone's rescue funding. At a summit on 29 June 2012, the European Council announced that Spanish banks would receive aid from the EFSF as soon as the details of EU-wide banking supervision were sorted out. Financial markets rejoiced[17] – until German finance minister Schäuble clarified later that he interpreted the agreement to mean that the Spanish government would be liable for the repayment of the funds borrowed.[18]

This exacerbated concerns over Madrid's ability to avoid a full bailout, and Spanish 10-year bond yields soared to new heights.[19] Germany's refusal to grant Spanish banks direct capital injections is rooted in the desire to break the cycle of 'financial assistance today in exchange for legal changes and clarity later'. Angela Merkel insisted on the creation of EU-wide banking supervision before providing more solidarity: 'If I am giving money to Spanish banks ... I am the German chancellor but I cannot say what these banks can do.'[20] The European governments are still working out the details of how direct bank recapitalizations will operate in principle. The Commission, however, is worried about more delay and the potential repercussions of not following through on already promised bank recapitalizations. Commission president José Manuel Barroso was eager to see an agreement on future direct European bank rescues before the German elections in September 2013. German anxiety about financial assistance first and legal clarity later is also reflected in the government's rejection of a debt redemption fund. Germany's Council of Economic Advisers suggested that such a fund could cover all public debts of member states above the ceiling of 60% laid down in the Maastricht treaty and would pay down the debt over 25 years. However, the Bundesbank doubted the compatibility of such a fund with European treaties or German constitutional law, warning that a mutualization of debts would lower the pressure on states with higher financing costs to engage in sound fiscal policies.[21]

Disputes over Instruments of Crisis-Fighting Measures

To avoid a major credit crunch and possible meltdown of Europe's banking system, the ECB injected 1 trillion euros of liquidity into the eurozone banking system, known as longer-term refinancing operations (LTROs), between December 2011 and March 2012.[22] In each case, the ECB's intervention led to a significant drop in the bond yields of troubled states.

The ECB's willingness to act as lender of last resort was praised by European leaders in the eurozone's periphery. But the bond-buying program triggered a controversial debate about the expansion of the ECB's mandate beyond the traditional inflation-fighting role. The German member of the ECB's board, Jürgen Stark, resigned following the ECB's decision to buy Italian and Spanish bonds in October 2011. Similarly, Axel Weber resigned his position as president of the German Bundesbank to protest against the ECB's bond-buying program, effectively throwing open the candidacy for president of the ECB. To Stark and Weber, the ECB's bond-buying program was tantamount to direct monetary financing of eurozone member states and therefore a violation of EU law. According to Mario Draghi, however, LTROs are within the ECB's mandate if bond risk premiums hamper the effectiveness of ECB monetary policy.[23]

Others have criticized the ECB's first intervention in bond markets between December 2011 and March 2012 as insufficient. De Grauwe[24] has argued that the LTROs were ineffective because the ECB intervened only indirectly in sovereign bond markets. Since EU treaties prohibit the ECB from intervening directly, the ECB decided to delegate the power to buy government bonds to the weak banks. But because the trembling banks channeled only a fraction of the liquidity they obtained from the ECB into the government bond markets and the real economy, the ECB had to pour much more liquidity into the system than if it had decided to intervene itself. Even ECB president Draghi lamented that the LTRO had not been successful in encouraging the banks to lend: 'Several months have passed and we see that credit flows remain weak.'[25] De Grauwe argues that a direct ECB intervention is a more effective way to restore bank lending, but acknowledges that longstanding German opposition to this idea may be difficult to overcome.[26]

Although ECB, national central bankers and European leaders joined Angela Merkel's calls for an EU-wide bank supervision, it is likely to take some time until political disagreements about the legal details of a banking union will be resolved. The main bone of contention concerns the ECB's credibility as guarantor for price stability and banking supervisor. In 2009, the Larosiere report recommended that the ECB assume responsibility for macro-prudential supervision (overall financial stability) but warned against giving it the power of micro-prudential supervision (individual banks). The main reason the authors counselled against micro-prudential supervision is that 'this could result in political pressure and interference, thereby jeopardizing the ECB's independence' (de Larosiere 2009, 43). According to the Larosiere group, but also the German Bundesbank, the LTROs effectively represented a rescue mechanism for weak banks, generating a conflict of interest: the ECB cannot credibly claim to maintain independence and price stability while at the same time helping weak banks and acting as the banks' supervisor.[27] However, the separation of macro- and micro-prudential supervision was suboptimal from an efficiency perspective: too many supervisory layers resulted in a delayed response to the banking crisis as national supervisors tended to underestimate the weakness of their national banks. Subsequent assessments of what a bank bailout might cost scared financial markets, driving up bond yields.[28]

Disputes over Conditionality of Financial Assistance

Pressing needs for emergency capital in the eurozone's large economies, in turn, fueled concerns among German policymakers that the conditions attached to financial assistance – structural reforms and austerity measures in the eurozone's troubled member states – were put at risk. Troika representatives have repeatedly criticized Greece for delays in implementing reforms, and eurozone ministers have threatened to withhold already promised aid to keep up the pressure on the government. In their fifth review report, troika officials acknowledged that the recession in Greece would be deeper than originally anticipated, but attributed Athens' failure to improve investor sentiment to delays in privatizations and structural reforms (European Central Bank 2011). In March 2012, Greece committed to cut the public debt to 120% of gross domestic product by 2020, but the programme has gone off track following Greece's tumultuous elections in May and June 2012. The troika therefore demanded that the governing coalition under Prime Minister Antonis Samaras come up with an additional 2.5 billion euros in savings to meet the 11.5 billion euro target set by the troika for 2013 and 2014.[29]

Structural reforms in the eurozone's troubled member states are likely to result in higher German inflation rates in the long run. German wage costs have lagged behind those in other eurozone countries for years. Workers acquiescence to wage moderation has boosted the competitiveness of German exports, but left southern Europe struggling to transform their stagnating economies. The IMF therefore suggested that more spending by German consumers should be encouraged, helping to generate demand for exports from other countries. According to the IMF, Germany is pivotal in reducing euro area and global imbalances.[30] As the eurozone's debt-ridden member states undertake adjustments to improve their competitiveness, upward pressure on German wage costs and property prices are likely to result in German inflation rates above the union's average. But the economic contraction in the periphery implies that those countries face downward price pressures, while Germany will have to live with higher inflation rates as a result of austerity.[31]

Unsurprisingly, the belt-tightening policies had been widely unpopular with the citizens in the affected countries. Austerity measures led to the collapse of governments in Ireland, Greece, Portugal and Italy and contributed to the defeat of governments in Spain and France. The election of French president Francois Hollande forced the German Chancellor to adopt a more pro-active policy to stimulate economic growth in the eurozone. European leaders saw this as an opportunity to renegotiate the rigid conditions of the financial assistance programmes and a chance to push for jointly issued euro bonds and other forms of shared debt. While Merkel agreed to a modification of the Fiscal Compact to add growth-boosting initiatives, she rejected calls for jointly issued euro bonds, declaring that 'Germany's strength is not infinite'.[32] Her statement came after mounting dissent in her governing coalition over the rising price tag of the bailouts and one month before Moody's changed its outlook for Germany's AAA credit rating to negative, the first step towards a possible downgrade, owing to the increased likelihood of a Greek exit from the euro and concerns that Spain will have to seek a full bailout.[33]

Since German policymakers had continuously defined the defence of the eurozone as a fundamental national interest, many worried that threats to withhold financial assistance to countries that did not fulfil reform promises were unconvincing. Consequently, political incumbents began to assert that a eurozone exit was a real possibility. The prospect of a Greek exit was first floated by the German finance minister after Greece's then Prime Minister Papandreou proposed to hold a referendum on the bailout in November 2011. The debate was rekindled after the first Greek election in May 2012, which produced stalemate, and continued after reform-willing political parties came to power in Athens in June 2012. After the IMF was rumoured to refuse further aid to Greece in July 2012, Germany's vice chancellor remarked that a Greek exit from the euro had long ceased to be a frightening prospect for him.[34]

Cyprus became the next flashpoint in crisis when the insolvency of the island's oversized banking sector briefly raised the specter of a new doctrine that would put the burden of future bank restructurings on depositors rather than taxpayers. While ESM funds had been used directly to recapitalize weak Spanish banks, there was no political willingness to rescue a 'money-laundering paradise' in this way. Bailout fatigue was particularly evident in Germany in light of the forthcoming 2013 federal elections. The initial proposal to introduce a tax on deposits, even those covered by the EU-wide deposit insurance, was withdrawn after the Cypriot parliament rejected it and several eurozone governments had loudly denounced the plan. After the ECB threatened to withhold emergency support for Cyprus' banks, a new agreement was reached wherein the ESM made 10 million euros available. In exchange, the two largest Cypriot banks were wound down. Depositors holding more than 100,000 euros at these institutions were expected to lose up to 60% of their funds, while deposits under this amount were spared. In order to prevent a massive outflow of euros, the Cypriot government introduced severe capital controls, the first eurozone country ever to do so. This measure breached one of the key pillars of the single currency.[35] While the instant risk of contagion receded, uncertainty over the broader ramifications of the Cyprus case kept the euro under pressure.

Relentless redenomination risk indicates that the eurozone crisis management failed to generate the EU's 'seal of approval' signal (Gray 2009). One might have expected consecutive bailouts by the member states and IMF, the creation of a permanent rescue fund, and subsequent boosts of the rescue fund's resources to lend credibility to the EU's 'no eurozone exit' declarations. However, the delayed response to the sovereign debt turmoil as well as permanent renegotiations of size, instruments and conditionality of financial assistance programs failed to reassure market participants, preventing the restoration of the 'EU glow'.

Conclusion

The eurozone debt drama constitutes the biggest shock in the history of European integration. The crisis is a particularly good case for examining informal governance in the EU as the eurozone was in a permanent state of emergency between 2009 and 2012. Rule violations occurred on an unprecedented scale, and emergency measures were crucially shaped by Germany while EU institutions took a back seat. However, Germany was unable to protect its core objectives – stabilizing the eurozone, limiting the taxpayers' financial guarantee load, and keeping inflation low. Germany's authority as creditor-in-chief, stability anchor and growth engine in the EU should have enabled political officials to safeguard these objectives. The fact that Germany failed to do so is inconsistent with the expectation of the informal governance literature that the dominant country will always be able to act on its core interests when the stakes are high and the costs of adhering to legal rule revision procedures are prohibitive.

We found that paying attention to temporal trade-offs in the study of informal governance allows us to capture incentives for short-sighted behaviour that helps explain this hitherto unexamined puzzle. We hypothesized that political leaders lack incentives to invest in addressing problems that seem manageable at first, but may cause escalating costs as they continue to fester. If an effective crisis resolution requires the dominant country to incur high upfront costs, but the principal responds to an incentive structure that rewards delay, the dominant agent may unintentionally sacrifice its core interests in the process. To restore investor confidence in the eurozone, Germany was under international pressure to provide credible backstops to shore up the bond markets of vulnerable member states on the brink of losing access to capital markets. However, policymakers responded to an incentive structure that rewarded crisis mitigation efforts rather than preparedness. This explains Germany's long hesitation before offering any financial assistance. Once Germany agreed to provide financial guarantees to its partners, political disagreements over the sequence of reform steps, instruments and conditionality of financial assistance programmes undermined the effectiveness of the rescue measures and increased the costs of stabilizing the eurozone.

Our finding is important for the literature on international institutions. It shows that the EU's power to confer investor confidence was limited to ordinary times. It fell apart when a reluctant hegemon tried to make the best of conflicting core interests, with market participants attempting to second-guess policymakers' intentions as well as capabilities. Our analysis suggests that German voters may consider investment in more large-scale eurozone rescue measures a public good only after the effects of contagion are palpable in Germany or once relentless debate of a eurozone exit make clear the costs of inaction. Alternatively, it is possible that self-fulfilling forces coalesce around a crisis outcome which leave the dominant country powerless to enforce its preferred policy solution.

Our analysis shows that attention to the hegemon's incentive structure can provide additional insights into the international and domestic trade-offs strong players face. Leading states are always confronted with competing pressures, but the dynamics of informal interactions are contingent upon how domestic audiences perceive the stakes of the game. Specifically, domestic audiences are less likely to worry about the dominant country's actions when the costs of a rule override are deferred into the future. However, when the immediate costs of informal governance are high and redistributive, domestic audiences are expected to be highly engaged and may constrain the hegemon's subsequent moves and room of maneuver. Future research may examine whether this finding carries to other international organizations in which the dominant player is subject to an incentive structure plagued by time-inconsistency problems.

Acknowledgements

For helpful comments and early conversations, I am grateful to Gabriel Gloeckler, Deborah Mabbett, Daniela Schwarzer, Martin Steinwand, Zoe Walker, the participants of the 2013 Midwest Political Science conference, the 2013 EUSA conference, two anonymous reviewers, and the students in my West European Politics seminar that was taught at Seton Hall University in Fall 2012. Financial support from the Fritz Thyssen foundation (Az. 50.11.0.010) is gratefully acknowledged

Notes

[1] Manokha and Chalabi (2011) have declared the international relations literature 'bankrupt' owing to the dearth of International Relations scholarship on the eurozone crisis.

[2] Regierungserklarung von Bundeskanzlerin Angela Merkel, 'Europa muss Stabilitatsunion werden', 26 October 2011. http://www.bundesregierung.de/Content/DE/Artikel/2011/10/2011-10-26-merkel-regierungserklaerung-er-euro.html.

[3] Redenomination risk signifies the fear that investors' deposits could be restated in units of a new currency that would devalue massively.

4 The troika consists of representatives of the European Commission, ECB and IMF.

5 Garrett (1993) has argued that political leaders facing substantial competitive slack are more willing to adopt policies that are not electorally optimal in the short run in order to achieve longer-term policy change.

6 I am not suggesting that the potential consequences of a eurozone breakup are equivalent to the destruction caused by a hurricane or flooding, as damage by the latter can be more easily repaired. However, the incentive structure politicians respond to is similar in both cases.

7 Statements by A. Merkel and N. Sarkozy, 11 February 2010, http://www.bundesregierung.de/Content/ DE/ Mitschrift/Pressekonferenzen/2010/02/2010–02–11-pk-europaeischer-rat.html.

8 'Germans say eurozone may have to expel Greece: poll', Reuters, 14 February 2010.

9 Only 80 billion euros are deposited in the ESM, the rest are financial guarantees. The biggest hurdle to the establishment of the EMS was cleared in September 2012 when the German constitutional court dismissed attempts to block it.

10 Germany agreed to provide 27% of EFSF financial guarantees. France provided 20, Italy 18 and Spain 12% of EFSF financial guarantees. EurActiv.de, October 2011.

11 'EFSF-Hilfen jetzt auch für Zypern und Spanien', EurActiv.de, 26 June 2012.

12 Radoslaw Sikorski, 'I fear Germanys power less than her inactivity', Financial Times, 28 November 2011.

13 Guy Verhofstadt, 'Germany knows way to solve crisis', Financial Times, 29 February 2012.

14 'I ultimately don't know whether Greece needs to leave the euro in order for the eurozone to do the things necessary to make their currency survive. I just don't know whether the German government requires Greek exit to explain to their public why they need to do certain things like a banking union, eurobonds and things in common with that' ('Germany Might Have to Sacrifice Greece to Save Euro, George Osborne Suggests',)Guardian, 12 June 2012.

15 Forschungsgruppe Wahlen, www.forschungsgruppe.de.

16 'Draghi Calls for EU-wide Bank Oversight', Financial Times, 31 May 2012.

17 'Markets Rebound after Eurozone Deal', Financial Times, 29 June 2012.

18 'Schauble wirbt für Milliardenhilfe für Spanien', Der Spiegel, 19 July 2012.

19 Spain's 10-year bond yields rose to 7.3%. 'Spains Borrowing Costs Soar', Financial Times, 20 July 2012.

20 'Eurozone Rift Deepens over Debt Crisis', Financial Times, 22 June 2012.

21 'Bundesbank Opposes Eurozone Debt Redemption Fund', EUbusiness, 18 June 2012.

22 In March 2012, the ECB discontinued the LTRO, asserting that it was now the eurozone governments' turn to implement more crisis-fighting measures. However, in July 2012 ECB president Mario Draghi announced that the programme would be reactivated after Spanish and Italian bond yields soared to levels that risk making borrowing unsustainable over the long term ('ECB "Ready to Do Whatever It Takes"', Financial Times, 26 July 2012).

23 'ECB "Ready to Do Whatever It Takes"', Financial Times, 26 July 2012.

24 Paul de Grauwe, 'Direct ECB Intervention Is Still the Only Way to End the Crisis', Financial Times, 13 March 2012.

25 'Draghi Running Out of Wiggle Room', Financial Times, 5 July 2012.

26 Paul de Grauwe, 'Direct ECB Intervention Is Still the Only Way to End the Crisis', Financial Times, 13 March 2012.

27 Othmar Issing, 'Europe's Political Union Is an Idea Worthy of Satire', Financial Times, 29 July 2012; Oliver Klasen, 'Draghi und Weidmann ringen um EZB-Linie', Sueddeutsche Zeitung, 30 July 2012.

28 'Draghi Calls for EU-wide Bank Oversight', Financial Times, 31 May 2012.

29 'Greece: Here We Go Again', CNN, 24 July 2012.

30 'Germany "Pivotal" to Rebalancing Eurozone', Financial Times, 3 July 2012.

31 'Bundesbank sieht keinen Anlass zur Panik', Handelsblatt, 10 May 2012.

32 Regierungserklarung von Bundeskanzlerin Merkel zum Europaischen Rat, 27 June 2012, Brussels, Belgium.

33 'Germany's AAA Credit Rating on Negative Outlook', BBC News, 24 July 2012.

34 'Rosler: Euro-Austritt Griechenlands hat Schrecken verloren', Focus, 22 July 2012.

35 'If Capital Controls Are Introduced in Cyprus, It Is the End of the Single Currency in All but Name,' Telegraph, 22 March 2013.

References

Alesina, A., and V. Grilli. 1991. "The European Central Bank: Reshaping Monetary Politics in Europe.", NBER Working Paper 3860; National Bureau of Economic Research.

de Larosiere, J. 2009. *DG Internal Market & DG Economic and Financial Affairs.* Brussels, Belgium: The High-Level Group on Financial Supervision in the EU.

European Central Bank. 2011. *Statement by the European Commission, the ECB and IMF on the Fifth Review Mission to Greece.* European Central Bank press release, 11 October 2011, Frankfurt am Main: Germany.

Fearon, J. D. 1995. "Rationalist Explanations for War." *International Organization* 49 (3): 379–414.

Featherstone, K. 2011. "The JCMS Annual Lecture: The Greek Sovereign Debt Crisis and EMU: A Failing State in a Skewed Regime." *Journal of Common Market Studies* 49 (2): 193–217.

Fligstein, N. 2008. *Euroclash: The EU, European Identity, and the Future of Europe.* Oxford, New York: Oxford University Press.

Garrett, G. 1993. "The Politics of Structural Change: Swedish Social Democracy and Thatcherism in Comparative Perspective." *Comparative Political Studies* 25 (4): 521–547.

Gartner, M., and B. Griesbach. 2012. "Rating Agencies, Self-Fulfilling Prophecy and Multiple Equilibria? An Empirical Model of the European Sovereign Debt Crisis 2009–2011.". Discussion Paper no. 2012-15, Universität St. Gallen.

Grabbe, H. 2001. "How Does Europeanization Affect CEE Governance? Conditionality, Diffusion and Diversity." *Journal of European Public Policy* 8 (6): 1013–1031.

Gray, J. 2009. "International Organization As a Seal of Approval: European Union Accession and Investor Risk." *American Journal of Political Science* 53 (4): 931–949.

Hall, P. A., and R. J. Franzese. 1998. "Mixed Signals: Central Bank Independence, Coordinated Wage Bargaining, and European Monetary Union." *International Organization* 52 (3): 505–535.

Healy, A., and N. Malhotra. 2009. "Myopic Voters and Natural Disaster Policy." *American Political Science Review* 103 (3): 387–406.

Heisenberg, D. 2006. "Merkel's EU Policy: "Kohl's Mädchen" or Interest-Driven Politics?" *German Politics and Society* 24 (1): 108–118.

Hennessy, A. 2011. "The Role of Agenda Setting in Pension Market Integration." *Journal of European Integration* 33 (5): 577–597.

Jacobs, A. M. 2011. *Governing for the Long Term: Democracy and the Politics of Investment.* Cambridge: Cambridge University Press.

Jones, E. 2010. "Merkel's Folly." *Survival* 52 (3): 21–38.

Kleine, M. 2013. "Knowing Your Limits: Informal Governance and Judgment in the European Union." *The Review of International Organizations* 8 (2): 245–264.

Koremenos, B. 2001. "Loosening the Ties That Bind: A Learning Model of Agreement Flexibility." *International Organization* 55 (2): 289–325.

Koremenos, B. 2005. "Contracting Around International Uncertainty." *American Political Science Review* 99 (4): 549–565.

Koremenos, B., C. Lipson, and D. Snidal. 2001. "The Rational Design of International Institutions." *International Organization* 55 (4): 761–799.

Krugman, P. 1996. *Are Currency Crises Self-Fulfilling? NBER Macroeconomics Annual 1996.* Vol. 11 National Bureau of Economic Research. Cambridge, MA: MIT Press.

Manokha, I., and M. Chalabi. 2011. "The Latest Financial Crisis: IR Goes Bankrupt.".

Matthijs, M., and M. Blyth. 2011. "Why Only Germany Can Fix the Euro." *Foreign Affairs.*

Obstfeld, M. 1994. "The Logic of Currency Crises.", NBER Working Paper 4640; National Bureau of Economic Research.

Öhler, H., P. Nunnenkamp, and A. Dreher. 2012. "Does Conditionality Work? A Test for An Innovative US Aid Scheme." *European Economic Review* 56 (3-4): 138–153.

Paterson, W. E. 2011. "The Reluctant Hegemon? Germany Moves Centre Stage in the European Union." *Journal of Common Market Studies* 49 (1): 57–75.

Pierson, P. 2004. *Politics in Time: History, Institutions, and Social Analysis.* Princeton, NJ: Princeton University Press.

Princen, S. 2009. *Agenda-Setting in the European Union.* London: Palgrave Macmillan.

Rosendorff, B. P. 2005. "Stability and Rigidity: Politics and Design of the WTO's Dispute Settlement Procedure." *American Political Science Review* 99 (3): 389–400.

Rosendorff, B. P., and H. V. Milner. 2001. "The Optimal Design of International Trade Institutions: Uncertainty and Escape." *International Organization* 55 (4): 829–857.

Sobel, R., and P. Leeson. 2006. "Government's Response to Hurricane Katrina: A Public Choice Analysis." *Public Choice* 127 (1-2): 55–73.

Stone, R. W. 2011. *Controlling Institutions: International Organizations and the Global Economy.* Cambridge: Cambridge University Press.

Tallberg, J. 2006. *Leadership and Negotiation in the European Union. Themes in European Governance.* Cambridge, New York: Cambridge University Press.

Thomson, R., F. N. Stokman, C. H. Achen, and T. König. 2006. *The European Union Decides. Testing Theories of European Decision-Making.* New York: Cambridge University Press.

Underdal, A. 1992. "Designing Politically Feasible Solutions." In *Rationality and Institutions,* edited by R. Malnes, and A. Underdal. Oslo: Scandinavian University Press.

Index

Academy of Finland 8–10, 12, 60–3, 73–4
accountability, concept of 65, 71–3
Åhnberg, Annika 29
Alapuro, R. 72
Alstadheim, Håvard 6
Altia (company) 53
Anscombe, Elizabeth 88
area studies 11, 16–17
austerity programmes 97, 105

bailouts 96–106
Bakhtin, Mikhail M. 11
Bank of England 96
Barroso, José Manuel 103
Blackburn, S. 87
Blåfeld, Antti 49–54
Blair, Tony 82
Børdahl, Amund 16
Brown, Chris 81
Bundesbank 96, 98, 103–4

Carlsson, Ingvar 25–6, 30
Carr, E.H. 89
categorical imperative 80
'chronotope' concept 11
'citizen-consumer' concept 67, 70, 73
civil society actors, criticisms of 52
climate change 71
'coach state' concept 60, 71, 73
commissions of inquiry 5–7, 36
communitarianism 81
competitiveness and the 'competition economy'
    46, 49–51, 54, 56, 66
'concrete society' 22
consequentialism 88
contagion, financial 97, 107
Copenhagen Criteria 96
Corner, J. 47
cosmopolitanism 81, 85
crisis management 98–9, 106–7
crisis mitigation 93–4, 98, 107

Crossley-Frolick, K.A. 85
Cyprus 100, 106

Dellinger, Misha 52
Delors, Jacques 38
democratic deficit 40
democratic processes 37, 41–2
Denmark 7–8, 35–43
deontology 88
Diez, T. 87
Draghi, Mario 104

Edenheim, S. 61
editorials in newspapers 48–54
emigration from Sweden 6
Engelstad, Fredrik 10, 40, 42
Enzensberger, Hans-Magnus 4–5
Eriksen, Erik 85–6, 88
Erkko, Eljas 49
Erlander, Tage 21–3
Esping, Hans 22
ethics of EU foreign policy 78–9
European Central Bank (ECB) 94, 96,
    103–6
European Economic Area (EEA) 38, 40–1
European Financial Stability Facility (EFSF)
    100, 102
European Free Trade Association (EFTA) 38
European integration 35–43, 95, 106; historical
    legacies bearing on 43
European Monetary Union (EMU) 38
European Security Strategy 84–5
European Stability Mechanism 100, 106
European Union (EU) 3, 30, 46; Charter of
    Fundamental Rights 84, 87; concepts of
    justice in the documentation of 84–6; foreign
    policy 76–90; moral agency of 83–4
Eurozone project 3, 55, 93–107

Fearon, J.D. 102
Finland 8–16, 42, 45–57, 60–75

'freedom of choice society' 21
Fukuyama, Francis 80–1

Gartner, M. 97
Gaskarth, J. 82
Germany 40–1; core interests of 93–7, 105–7; response to debt crisis 101–7
Global Justice Movement (GJM) 49, 52
globalisation 39, 41, 45, 49–56; critics of 52–3
Götz, Norbert 73
Gray, J. 97
Greece 86, 95–102, 105–6
Griesbach, B. 97

Haapala, Pertti 64, 69–70
Halonen, Tarja 53
Hämäläinen, T. 46
Hegel, G.W.F. 55
hegemonic financial position 93–5
hegemonic ideology 50
Heimskringla 1, 5
Heiskala, Risto 46, 64, 67, 71–2
Helkama, Klaus 67
Helsingin Sanomat (*HS*) (newspaper) 45–56; as a power centre 48–9
Henningsen, Bernd 5
Hermansson, C.H. 24–5, 31
Hernes, Gudmund 6, 16
Heslsingin Sanomat (newspaper) 64
Hirdman, Yvonne 7, 26–9
Hollande, François 105
Honoré, Tony 86
human rights 40, 85–6
humanistic analysis 10
Humboldt, Wilhelm von 11
Hyde-Price, Adrian 86

Iceland 10
immigration 68
incomes policy 51
individualism 67, 72–3
informal governance theory 93–5, 106–7
'inquiry prose' 12
institutions, MacIntyre's view of 83
international institutions 67, 69, 73, 93, 107
international law 40, 86
International Monetary Fund (IMF) 96, 102, 105–6
internationalisation 39–43
intertextuality 11
investigative journalism 50, 56
Ireland 102
'iron triangles' 26, 30
Isotalus, Päivi 53
Italy 97

Jääsaari, J. 67
journalism, role of 45–50, 56
justice: as conceptualised in EU documentation 84–6; theory of 79–82, 89

Kagan, Robert 77
Kalela, J. 69
Kansan Uutiset (newspaper) 56
Kant, Immanuel 77–80
Kantianism 76–81, 87–8; *see also* neo-Kantianism
Kantola, Anu 64, 67, 71–2
Karvonen, Lauri 69
Katrineholm Study 27
Kettunen, P. 55
Kivinen, Olli 52, 54
Koivunen, Anu 67–8
Kunelius, R. 48

Labour Party, Norwegian 6
Lane, Jan-Erik 28
Lapintie, Kimmo 67, 69
Larosiere Report (2009) 104
legal systems 39–40
Lehtonen, Mikko 67–8
Lippmann, Walter 71
Lisbon Treaty 84, 96
literary theory 12
longer-term refinancing operations (LTROs) 103–4
Lönnroth, Måns 22, 26
Lordi (rock band) 71
Luhmann, Niklas 15
Lundqvist, Lennart J. 23

Maastricht Treaty 41, 96
MacIntyre, Alexander 76–8, 82–3, 88–9
majority voting in the EU 39
mandates for negotiations with the EU 42
Mani, Rama 81, 84
Manners, Ian 79, 86–9
market-oriented approach to the economy 51
Marx, Groucho 4
Marxism 63–4
media, the: functionalist concept of 15; role of 55
'mediatisation' 47
Merkel, Angela 95, 99–104
meta-ethics 79, 87
Meyer, Siri 8
Mill, John Stuart 57
M'kapa, Benjamin 53
Molin, Rune 22–3
moral claims 89

nation-states, role and power of 39, 46
national interests 54–5

neo-colonialism 77–9, 86–9
neo-Kantianism 77, 86–9
neo-liberalism 25, 46, 49, 51
newspapers, importance of 48
normative power, concept of 87
Norway 8, 11–13, 16, 25, 29, 35–43, 74

Olsen, Johan P. 6–7, 26
open economy 46
open society 21, 30–1, 36
Osborne, George 101
Østerud, Øyvind 8, 10, 15, 40, 42

Palme, Olof 25, 30
Papandreou, George 105
parliamentary control over policy 42–3
Partanen, Juha 63–6
Persson, Inga 7, 26
Petersson, Olof 7, 22, 26–8
Pietikäinen, Petteri 12, 62–72
politico-cultural practice, concept of 10–16
populist politicians 67, 72
Portugal 102
postmodern individualism 67
poststructuralism 12
power, power of investigation of 20–1
'power investigations' 1–15, 24–32, 35–40, 43,
    45, 61, 70, 73; function of 13, 15;
    intermediality of 13; by journalists 46–7; as
    politico-cultural practice 10–16; two-fold
    objective of 20–1
'practices' in foreign policy, definition of 82
'preparedness' spending by financial authorities
    98, 107
problem-solving capacity of states and
    international institutions 39–40, 43
'prosumers' 67, 69, 73
public opinion 71

rationalism 78–9
referenda in Nordic countries on European
    integration 36, 38
Rolf, Eckard 13
Romanticism 11
Rothstein, B. 27
rule-based morality 78
rule of law 81–5
Ruostetsaari, I. 67
Ruuskanen, O.-P. 69

Saari, J. 64
Samaras, Antonis 105
Schäuble, Wolfgang 103
Schengen area 38

Selle, P. 40, 42
Skjeie, Hege 8
Snellman, J.V. (and 'Snellmanian discourse')
    55
social democracy 20–5, 30–2
social justice 84, 86
sovereignty 39–43
Spain 97, 100–6
Stability and Growth Pact 96
Stark, Jürgen 104
stereotypes, use of 72
Stone, R.W. 93–5
'strong society' 21–2
'structural rationalisation' 22
Sturluson, Snorri 5
Sulkunen, Pekka 63–4
Sundbärg, Gustav 6
Suomen Akatemia 13
Svensson, Jörn 24
Svensson, Olle 24
Sweden 4–7, 16, 20–32, 35–8, 41–3, 61

TANDEM research programme 8, 60–8, 72–3;
    critics of 63
Tarschy, Daniel 24
Therborn, Göran 29
Thucydides 5
Togeby, Lise 7, 40
Toresson, Bo 23
transitional justice 84–5
'troika' arrangement 105
truth claims 13
Tsakatika, M. 82

Uimonen, Risto 53
universalism, moral 76, 78

Väliverronen, E. 47
VALTA programme 2, 45, 60–74; conclusions
    of 66; goals of 61–2
Valta Suomessa anthology (2010) 60–73
Virkkunen, Janne 49–51, 54, 56
virtue ethics 76–83, 86–9
Voegelin, Eric 5

Weber, Axel 104
welfare state provision 20–6, 29–32, 35, 37, 46,
    60, 70–1; cutbacks in 30–2
Westermarck Society 8
Whitman, R.G. 79
Widgrén, M. 69
Wright, Georg Henrik von 63

Ylä-Anttila, T. 72

For Product Safety Concerns and Information please contact our EU
representative GPSR@taylorandfrancis.com Taylor & Francis Verlag GmbH,
Kaufingerstraße 24, 80331 München, Germany

Batch number: 08153807

Printed by Printforce, the Netherlands